Rick Steves®

POCKET

VIENNA

Rick Steves with Gene Openshaw

Contents

Introduction

Vienna is the capital of Austria, the cradle of classical music, and one of the world's most livable cities. The city center is skyscraper free, pedestrian-friendly, and traversed by electric trams. It retains an 18th- and 19th-century elegance, when the city was at the forefront of the arts and sciences.

Today's Vienna—or Wien ("Voon")—is a modern city of 1.8 million. With world-class museums and sights such as St. Stephen's Cathedral and the Hofburg Palace, there's plenty to keep a sightseer busy. But compared with most urban centers, the pace of life here is slow. People nurse a pastry and coffee over the daily paper at small cafés. They sip wine under the stars, enjoy Mozart operas and Strauss waltzes, and continually work to perfect their knack for good living. Anyone with an interest in the arts, beautiful objects, or Sacher torte with whipped cream will feel right at home.

Introduction

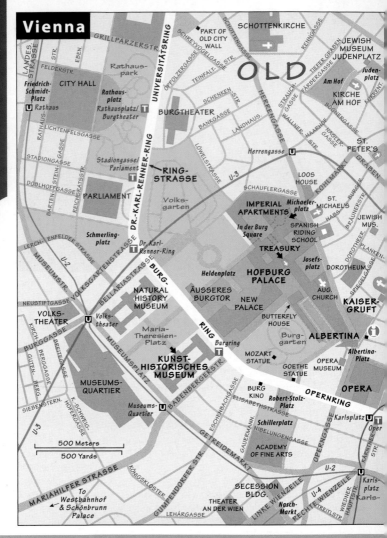

Vienna

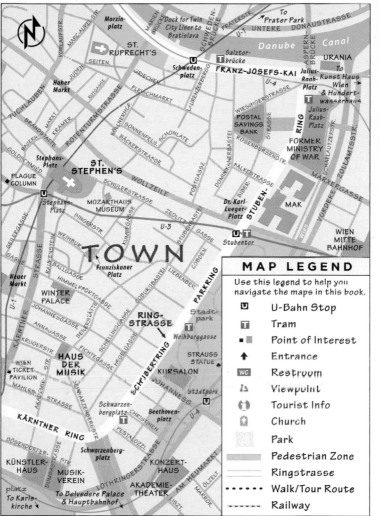

MAP LEGEND

Use this legend to help you navigate the maps in this book.

Ⓤ	U-Bahn Stop
Ⓣ	Tram
▪■	Point of Interest
↟	Entrance
WC	Restroom
⅄	Viewpoint
⋔	Tourist Info
✚	Church
▓	Park
	Pedestrian Zone
	Ringstrasse
⋯⋯	Walk/Tour Route
┄┄	Railway

About This Book

I've selected only the best of Vienna—admittedly, a tough call. The core of the book is seven self-guided walks and tours that zero in on Vienna's greatest sights and neighborhoods. The Vienna City Walk takes you through the heart of the city, while the Ringstrasse Tram Tour circles its elegant border. St. Stephen's Cathedral is a journey into Vienna's medieval past. At the Hofburg Palace, you're immersed in the Habsburg world—the opulent rooms of their Imperial Apartments and the crown jewels of the Treasury. The Kunsthistorisches Museum has some of the world's greatest paintings, from Titian to Rembrandt to Bruegel. Finally, there's a visit to Schönbrunn Palace, which combines beautiful art with the beauties of nature.

The rest of the book is a traveler's tool kit. You'll find plenty more about Vienna's attractions, from shopping to nightlife to less touristy sights. And there are helpful hints on saving money, avoiding crowds, getting around on Vienna's public transit, finding a great meal, and much more.

If you'd like more information than this Pocket Guide offers, I've sprinkled the book liberally with web references. For general travel tips—as well as updates to this book—see www.ricksteves.com/update.

Key to This Book

Sights are rated:

▲▲▲ **Don't miss**
▲▲ **Try hard to see**
▲ **Worthwhile if you can make it**
No rating **Worth knowing about**

Tourist information offices are abbreviated as **TI,** and bathrooms are **WCs.**

Like Europe, this book uses the **24-hour clock.** It's the same through 12:00 noon, then keep going: 13:00 (1:00 p.m.), 14:00 (2:00 p.m.), and so on. For opening times, if a sight is listed as "May-Oct daily 9:00-16:00," it's open from 9 a.m. until 4 p.m. from the first day of May until the last day of October.

Vienna Neighborhoods

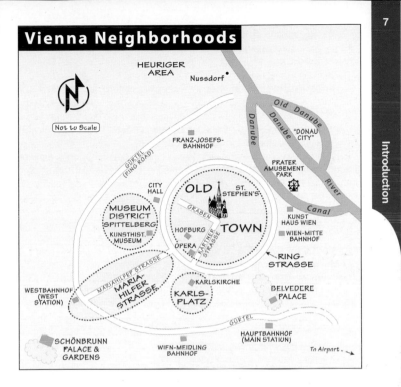

HEURIGER AREA

Nussdorf

Old Danube

Danube

Danube "DONAU CITY"

River

Not to Scale

GÜRTEL (RING ROAD)

FRANZ-JOSEFS-BAHNHOF

PRATER AMUSEMENT PARK

CITY HALL

OLD ST. STEPHEN'S

MUSEUM DISTRICT SPITTELBERG

GRABEN

Canal

KUNST HAUS WIEN

KUNSTHIST. MUSEUM

HOFBURG

TOWN

WIEN-MITTE BAHNHOF

OPERA

KÄRTNER STRASSE

RING-STRASSE

MARIAHILFER STRASSE

MARIA-HILFER STRASSE

KARLSKIRCHE

BELVEDERE PALACE

WESTBAHNHOF (WEST STATION)

KARLS-PLATZ

GÜRTEL

SCHÖNBRUNN PALACE & GARDENS

WIEN-MEIDLING BAHNHOF

HAUPTBAHNHOF (MAIN STATION)

To Airport

Vienna by Neighborhood

Vienna sits between the Vienna Woods (Wienerwald) and the Danube River (Donau). Think of the city map as a target with concentric circles: The bull's-eye is St. Stephen's Cathedral. Surrounding the old town is the grand circular boulevard called the Ringstrasse. The Gürtel, a broader, later ring road, contains the rest of downtown. Outside the Gürtel lies the uninteresting sprawl of modern Vienna.

Think of Vienna as a collection of neighborhoods:

Old Town (Within the Ring): Much of Vienna's sightseeing is located within the Ringstrasse. Here you'll find St. Stephen's Cathedral, the Hofburg complex, the opera house, and many great shops and restaurants.

St. Stephen's stands proudly in the center, at the intersection of the two main (pedestrian-only) streets: Kärntner Strasse and the Graben. To walk across the old town—say, from the opera house in the south to the Danube Canal in the north—takes about 30 minutes.

Ringstrasse: The ring road enclosing the old town is the former city wall. Now it's lined with grand buildings, such as the Rathaus (City Hall). Trams #1, #2, and #D travel along the Ring (which also has several stops for Vienna's subway—the U-Bahn), making the Ring a handy jumping-off point for sights located just inside or outside it.

Karlsplatz: The U-Bahn stop Karlsplatz (tram stop: Oper) is a major transportation hub on the Ring. Stretching south of here is a cluster of sights, including Karlskirche, Naschmarkt, the Secession, and Belvedere Palace.

Museum District: Just west of the Ring lies this classy area with the Kunsthistorisches art museum and several lesser galleries (the MuseumsQuartier). The pleasant student-oriented neighborhood of Spittelberg is great for cafés and nightlife.

Mariahilfer Strasse: Stretching still farther southwest is this mile-long street running from the Ring to the Westbahnhof (train station), linked by a string of convenient U-Bahn stops. This lively corridor has major department stores, medium-range eateries, and many of my recommended (and best-value) hotels. The east end of the street is nicer—close to downtown and the Museum District. The west end near the train station is a little rough around the edges.

Greater Vienna: Though not a "neighborhood" at all, these widely scattered sights are nevertheless easily connected by public transit.

Greater Vienna has Prater Park...

...and Schönbrunn, the royal summer palace.

Daily Reminder

Daily: The Haus der Musik is half-price after 20:00.

Sunday: All recommended sights and most tourist shops are open, but department stores and other shops are closed, including the Naschmarkt open-air market and the Dorotheum auction house. Most churches have restricted hours for sightseers, and there are no crypt tours at St. Michael's Church. The Spanish Riding School's Lipizzaner stallions usually perform at 11:00.

Monday: Most of the major sights are open (such as St. Stephen's Cathedral, Vienna State Opera, Hofburg Imperial Apartments and Treasury, Schönbrunn Palace, and Belvedere Palace), but many sights are closed, including the New Palace museums, the Secession, Academy of Fine Arts, and Imperial Furniture Collection. The Kunsthistorisches Museum is closed except in summer.

Tuesday: All sights are open, except the Hofburg Treasury, New Palace museums, and Natural History Museum.

Wednesday: All sights are open. The Albertina and Natural History Museum stay open until 21:00.

Thursday: All sights are open. The Kunsthistorisches and MuseumsQuartier museums stay open until 21:00.

Friday: All sights are open.

Saturday: All sights are open. The Spanish Riding School's Lipizzaner stallions usually perform at 11:00.

Vienna at a Glance

▲▲▲Hofburg Imperial Apartments Lavish main residence of the Habsburgs. **Hours:** Daily 9:00-17:30, July-Aug until 18:00. See page 122.

▲▲▲Hofburg Treasury The Habsburgs' collection of jewels, crowns, and other valuables—the best on the Continent. **Hours:** Wed-Mon 9:00-17:30, closed Tue. See page 122.

▲▲▲St. Stephen's Cathedral Enormous, historic Gothic cathedral in the center of Vienna. **Hours:** Foyer and north aisle—daily 6:00-22:00 (from 7:00 on Sun); main nave—Mon-Sat 9:00-11:30 & 13:00-16:30, Sun 13:00-16:30, June-Aug until 18:30. See page 127.

▲▲▲Vienna State Opera Dazzling, world-famous opera house. **Hours:** By guided tour only, July-Aug generally Mon-Sat at the top of hour 10:00-16:00, fewer tours Sept-June and Sun. See page 127.

▲▲▲Kunsthistorisches Museum World-class exhibit of the Habsburgs' art collection, including works by Raphael, Titian, Caravaggio, Rembrandt, and Bruegel. **Hours:** Daily 10:00-18:00, Thu until 21:00, closed Mon Sept-May. See page 129.

▲▲▲Schönbrunn Palace Spectacular summer residence of the Habsburgs, rivaling the grandeur of Versailles. **Hours:** Daily 8:30-17:30, July-Aug until 18:30, Nov-March until 17:00. See page 139.

▲▲Hofburg New Palace Museums Uncrowded collection of armor, musical instruments, and ancient Greek statues in the elegant halls of a Habsburg palace. **Hours:** Wed-Sun 10:00-18:00, closed Mon-Tue. See page 122.

▲▲Albertina Museum Habsburg residence with state apartments, world-class collection of graphic arts and modernist classics, and first-rate special exhibits. **Hours:** Daily 10:00-18:00, Wed until 21:00. See page 124.

▲▲Kaisergruft Crypt for Habsburg royalty. **Hours:** Daily 10:00-18:00. See page 125.

▲▲Haus der Musik Modern museum with interactive exhibits on Vienna's favorite pastime. **Hours:** Daily 10:00-22:00. See page 128.

▲▲**Natural History Museum** Big, beautiful catalog of the natural world, featuring the ancient *Venus of Willendorf*. **Hours:** Wed 9:00-21:00, Thu-Mon 9:00-18:30, closed Tue. See page 129.

▲▲**Belvedere Palace** Elegant palace of Prince Eugene of Savoy, with a collection of 19th- and 20th-century Austrian art (including Klimt). **Hours:** Daily 10:00-18:00, Lower Palace until 21:00 on Wed. See page 133.

▲**Spanish Riding School** Prancing white Lipizzaner stallions. **Hours:** Performances nearly year-round, usually Sat-Sun at 11:00, plus training sessions generally Tue-Fri 10:00-12:00. See page 123.

▲**St. Michael's Church Crypt** Final resting place of about 100 wealthy 18th-century Viennese. **Hours:** By tour Mon-Sat at 11:00 and 13:00, no tours Sun. See page 127.

▲**St. Peter's Church** Beautiful Baroque church in the old center. **Hours:** Mon-Fri 7:00-20:00, Sat-Sun 9:00-21:00. See page 128.

▲**Karlskirche** Baroque church offering the unique chance to ride an elevator up into the dome. **Hours:** Mon-Sat 9:00-18:00, Sun 13:00-19:00. See page 131.

▲**Academy of Fine Arts Painting Gallery** Small but exciting collection by 15th- to 18th-century masters. **Hours:** Tue-Sun 10:00-18:00, closed Mon. See page 131.

▲**The Secession** Art Nouveau exterior and Klimt paintings in situ. **Hours:** Tue-Sun 10:00-18:00, closed Mon. See page 132.

▲**Naschmarkt** Sprawling, lively outdoor market. **Hours:** Mon-Fri 6:00-18:30, Sat until 17:00, closed Sun, closes earlier in winter. See page 132.

▲**Kunst Haus Wien Museum** Modern art museum dedicated to zany local artist Hundertwasser. **Hours:** Daily 10:00-18:00. See page 135.

▲**Imperial Furniture Collection** Eclectic collection of Habsburg furniture. **Hours:** Tue-Sun 10:00-18:00, closed Mon. See page 138.

less than 30 minutes away from the *Heuriger* wine gardens (to the
Belvedere Palace (to the south), Prater amusement park (east), and
brunn Palace (southwest).

Planning Your Time

The following day-plans give an idea of how much an organized, moti-
vated, and caffeinated person can see.

Day 1: Circle the Ringstrasse on my self-guided tram tour, then tour
the Vienna State Opera (the tram tour starts/ends there). After lunch, follow
my Vienna City Walk, including visits to the Kaisergruft and St. Stephen's
Cathedral. Catch a Red Bus City Tour for a look at greater Vienna.

Day 2: Browse the colorful Naschmarkt. Tour the Kunsthistorisches
Museum. In the afternoon, tour the Hofburg Palace Imperial Apartments
and Treasury. Enjoy a leisurely dinner, or take in a concert or opera.

Day 3: Visit Belvedere Palace, with its fine Viennese art and great
city views. After lunch, take the U-Bahn out to Schönbrunn Palace. In the
evening, visit a *Heuriger* wine garden or enjoy another concert.

Day 4: Enjoy the engaging Karlsplatz sights (Karlskirche, Academy of
Fine Arts, and the Secession). Then do some shopping along Mariahilfer
Strasse, or rent a bike and head out to the modern Donau City downtown
sector, Danube Island, and Prater Park.

With More Time: There are plenty more sights to choose from in
Vienna. For suggestions, see the Sights chapter (as well as the "Activities"
on page 183).

These are busy day-plans, so be sure to schedule in slack time for
picnics, laundry, people-watching, leisurely dinners, concerts, café-sitting,
shopping, and recharging your touristic batteries. Slow down and be open
to unexpected experiences and the courtesy of the Austrian people.

Quick Tips: Reserve your hotel as soon as possible for summer
travel. To avoid long lines at a few sights, consider booking online or buying combo-tickets. Take advantage of my free Vienna audio tours, covering
three of this book's sights. (For more details, see page 180.)

And finally, remember that—although Vienna's sights can be crowded
and stressful—the city itself is all about gentility and grace, so...be flexible.

Have a great trip!

Vienna City Walk

Vienna, one of Europe's grandest cities of the past, is also a vibrant city of today. On this walk, we'll lace together the city's three most important landmarks. We start at the opera house, ground zero for Vienna's international reputation for classical music. Next is St. Stephen's Cathedral, with its skyscraping spire, the symbol of the city. We end at the Hofburg Palace—once the home of the Habsburgs, now brimming with top-notch museums.

Along the way, we'll be right in the thick of Vienna of today. It's a laidback world of genteel shops, cafés, chocolate, and Sacher torte. It's the city where the Viennese continually perfect their knack for good living.

This walk is a great first look at the city. Use it to get the lay of the land and an overview of sights you may want to explore more in depth later. It's a sampler of the best of Vienna—past and present.

This Walk: Allow one hour for the walk alone; more if you tour many of the major sights.

When to Go: This walk works just as well in the evening as it does during the day, as long as you don't plan on touring some of the sights you'll pass.

Opera House: A visit is possible only with a 45-minute guided tour (see page 185).

Albertina Museum: €13, daily 10:00-18:00, Wed until 21:00.

Kaisergruft: €5.50, daily 10:00-18:00.

St. Stephen's Cathedral: Church foyer and north aisle—free, daily 6:00-22:00 (from 7:00 on Sun); main nave—€4.50, Mon-Sat 9:00-11:30 & 13:00-16:30, Sun 13:00-16:30, June-Aug until 18:30. The cathedral's towers, catacombs, and treasury have varying costs and hours (see page 31).

St. Peter's Church: Free; Mon-Fri 7:00-20:00, Sat-Sun 9:00-21:00; free organ concerts Mon-Fri at 15:00, Sat-Sun at 20:00.

St. Michael's Church Crypt: €7 for 45-minute tour, Mon-Sat at 11:00 and 13:00, none on Sun.

Hofburg Imperial Apartments: €14, covered by Sisi Ticket (see page 180); daily 9:00-17:30, July-Aug until 18:00, last entry one hour before closing.

Hofburg Treasury: €12, €20 combo-ticket with Kunsthistorisches Museum, Wed-Mon 9:00-17:30, closed Tue.

Tours: 🎧 Download my free Vienna City Walk audio tour.

Starring: Vienna's "big three" (opera house, cathedral, palace), plus an array of sights, squares, and shops tucked between them.

THE WALK BEGINS

▶ *Begin at the square outside Vienna's landmark opera house, home of the Vienna State Opera (U-Bahn stop: Karlsplatz).*

① Opera House

If Vienna is the world capital of classical music, this building is its throne room. It's typical of Vienna's 19th-century buildings in that it features a revival style—Neo Renaissance—with arched windows, half-columns, and the sloping, copper mansard roof typical of French Renaissance *châteaux*.

Since the structure was built in 1869, almost all of the opera world's luminaries have passed through here. Its former musical directors include Gustav Mahler, Herbert von Karajan, and Richard Strauss. Luciano Pavarotti, Maria Callas, Placido Domingo, and many other greats have sung from its stage.

In the pavement along the side of the opera house (and all along Kärntner Strasse, the bustling shopping street we'll visit shortly), you'll find star plaques forming a Hollywood-style walk of fame. These represent the stars of classical music—famous composers, singers, musicians, and conductors. Looking up at the opera, notice the giant outdoor screen onto which some live performances are projected (as noted in the posted schedules and on the screen itself).

The opera's interior is sumptuous, but to see it you'll have to attend a performance (see page 185) or take a guided tour (see page 127 for details).

The opera house marks a busy intersection in Vienna, where Kärntner

The opera house was built for royalty…   …but commoners enjoy the live video feed.

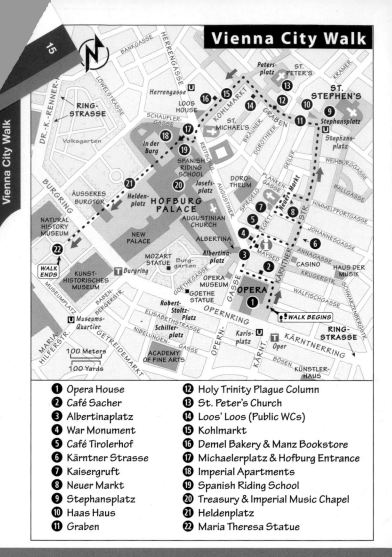

Vienna City Walk

- ❶ Opera House
- ❷ Café Sacher
- ❸ Albertinaplatz
- ❹ War Monument
- ❺ Café Tirolerhof
- ❻ Kärntner Strasse
- ❼ Kaisergruft
- ❽ Neuer Markt
- ❾ Stephansplatz
- ❿ Haas Haus
- ⓫ Graben
- ⓬ Holy Trinity Plague Column
- ⓭ St. Peter's Church
- ⓮ Loos' Loos (Public WCs)
- ⓯ Kohlmarkt
- ⓰ Demel Bakery & Manz Bookstore
- ⓱ Michaelerplatz & Hofburg Entrance
- ⓲ Imperial Apartments
- ⓳ Spanish Riding School
- ⓴ Treasury & Imperial Music Chapel
- ㉑ Heldenplatz
- ㉒ Maria Theresa Statue

Strasse meets the Ring. The Karlsplatz U-Bahn station in front of the opera is an underground shopping mall with fast food, newsstands, and lots of pickpockets.

▶ *Walk behind the opera and across the street toward the dark-red awning to find the famous...*

❷ Café Sacher

This is the home of the world's classiest chocolate cake, the Sacher torte: two layers of cake separated by apricot jam and covered in dark-chocolate icing, usually served with whipped cream. It was invented in a fit of improvisation in 1832 by Franz Sacher, dessert chef to Prince Metternich (the mastermind diplomat who redrew the map of post-Napoleonic Europe). The cake became world famous when the inventor's son served it next door at his hotel (you may have noticed the fancy doormen). Many locals complain that the cakes here have gone downhill, and many tourists are surprised by how dry they are—you really need that dollop of *Schlagobers*. Still, coffee and a slice of cake here can be €8 well invested for the history alone (daily 8:00-24:00). While the café itself

Break time. Sacher torte, supposedly invented here, comes with whipped cream, or *Schlagobers*.

is grotesquely touristy, the adjacent Sacher Stube has ambience and na-
tives to spare (same prices, daily 10:00-24:00). For maximum elegance,
sit inside.

▶ *Continue past Hotel Sacher. At the end of the street is a small, triangular,*
cobbled square adorned with memorial sculptures. (As you approach
*the square, to the right you'll find the **TI**; see page 172.)*

❸ Albertinaplatz

On the left, the tan-and-white Neoclassical building with the statue alcoves
marks the tip of the Hofburg Palace—the sprawling complex of buildings
that was long the seat of Habsburg power. The balustraded terrace up top
was the balcony of Empress Maria Theresa's daughter Maria Christina,
who lived here. Today, her home houses the **Albertina Museum,** topped
by a sleek titanium canopy (called the "diving board" by critics). The museum's plush, 19th-century state rooms are the only Neoclassical (post-
Rococo) palace rooms anywhere in the Habsburg realm. And the Batliner
Collection of modernist paintings (Monet to Picasso) is a delight (see page
125).

Albertinaplatz itself has the powerful ❹ **Monument Against War
and Fascism,** which commemorates the dark years when Austria came
under Nazi rule (1938-1945). The memorial has four parts. The split white
Gates of Violence brings to mind the gates of a concentration camp. Other
parts of the monument present a montage of wartime images: clubs, WWI
gas masks, a dying woman birthing a future soldier, victims of cruel medical experimentation, and chained slave laborers on a pedestal of gran-
ite cut from the infamous quarry at Mauthausen concentration camp.
The hunched-over figure on the ground behind is a Jew forced to scrub

Dive into art at the Albertina Museum.

A stark reminder of the Fascist years

anti-Nazi graffiti off a street with a brush. Of Vienna's 200,000 Jews, more than 65,000 died in Nazi concentration camps. The sculpture with its head buried in the stone reminds Austrians of the horrible consequences of turning a blind eye to the fascist threat.

Viewing this monument gains even more emotional impact when you realize what happened on this spot: During a WWII bombing attack, several hundred people were buried alive when their cellar shelter was demolished.

Austria was led into World War II by Germany, which annexed the country in 1938, saying Austrians were wannabe Germans anyway. But Austrians are not Germans—never were, never will be. Near the back of the square stands the declaration that established a democratic Austria in 1945, and once again restored the country's basic human rights.

Behind the monument is ⑤ **Café Tirolerhof,** a classic Viennese café. It's full of things that time has passed by: chandeliers, marble tables, upholstered booths, waiters in tuxes, and newspapers. For more on Vienna's cafés, see page 156.

This square is where many of the city's walking tours and bus tours start, including Red Bus City Tours (see page 190).

▶ *From the café, turn right on Führichsgasse. Walk one block until you hit...*

⑥ Kärntner Strasse

This grand, traffic-free street is the people-watching delight of this in-love-with-life city. In the 19th century, it was lined with some of Vienna's most elegant shops. Today's Kärntner Strasse is mostly a crass commercial pedestrian mall—its famed elegant shops are long gone. But locals know it's the same road Crusaders marched down as they headed off from St. Stephen's Cathedral for the Holy Land in the 12th century. Today it's full of shoppers and street musicians.

As you walk, be sure to look up, above the modern storefronts, for glimpses of the street's former glory. On the left at #26, **J & L Lobmeyr Crystal** ("Founded in 1823"), still has its impressive brown storefront with gold trim, statues, and the Habsburg double-eagle. In the market for some $400 napkin rings? Lobmeyr's your place. Inside, breathe in the classic Old World ambience as you climb up to the glass museum (free entry, closed Sun).

▶ *At the end of the block, turn left on Marco d'Aviano Gasse (passing the fragrant flower stall) to make a short detour to the square called Neuer*

From the opera house to the cathedral, Kärntner Strasse cuts through the center of Vienna.

Markt. Straight ahead is an orange-ish church with a triangular roof and cross, the Capuchin Church. In its basement is the...

❼ Kaisergruft

Under the church sits the Imperial Crypt, filled with what's left of Austria's emperors, empresses, and other Habsburg royalty. For centuries, Vienna was the heart of a vast empire ruled by the Habsburg family, and here is where they lie buried in their fancy pewter coffins. You'll find all the Habsburg greats, including Maria Theresa, her son Josef II (Mozart's patron), Franz Josef, and Empress Sisi. Before moving on, consider paying your respects here (see page 125).

▶ *Stretching north from the Kaisergruft is the square called...*

❽ Neuer Markt

In the center of Neuer Markt is the **four rivers fountain** showing Lady Providence surrounded by figures symbolizing the rivers that flow into the Danube. The sexy statues offended Empress Maria Theresa, who actually organized "Chastity Commissions" to defend her capital city's moral standards.

The modern buildings around you were rebuilt after World War II. Half of the city's inner center was intentionally destroyed by Churchill to demoralize the Viennese, who were disconcertingly enthusiastic about the Nazis.

▶ *Lady Providence's one bare breast points back to Kärntner Strasse. Turn left and continue down Kärntner Strasse. As you approach the cathedral, you're likely to first see it as a reflection in the round-glass windows of the postmodern Haas Haus. Pass the U-Bahn station (which has WCs) where the street spills into Vienna's main square.*

❾ Stephansplatz

The cathedral's frilly spire looms overhead, worshippers and tourists pour inside the church, and shoppers buzz around the outside. You're at the center of Vienna.

The Gothic **St. Stephen's Cathedral** (c. 1300-1450) is known for its 450-foot south tower, its colorful roof, and its place in Viennese history. When it was built, it was a huge church for what was then a tiny town, and it helped put the fledgling city on the map. At this point, you may want to take a break from the walk to tour the church (✪ see the St. Stephen's Cathedral Tour chapter).

St. Stephen's glorious 700-year history…   …is reflected in this modern building.

Facing St. Stephen's, the sleek concrete-and-glass ⑩ **Haas Haus** (1990, by noted Austrian architect Hans Hollein) has a curved facade meant to echo the Roman fortress of Vindobona (its ruins were found near here). Once controversial, it's become a fixture. The glass reflection of St. Stephen's is a great photo opportunity, especially at twilight. The café and pricey restaurant on the rooftop offer a nice perch (take the elevator to the sixth floor, and walk up one flight to the terrace).

▶ *Exit the square with your back to the cathedral. Walk past the Haas Haus, and bear right down the street called the…*

⑪ Graben

This was once a *Graben,* or ditch—originally the moat for the Roman military camp. Back during Vienna's 19th-century heyday, there were nearly 200,000 people packed into the city's inner center (inside the Ringstrasse), walking through dirt streets. Today this area houses 20,000. The Graben was a busy street with three lanes of traffic until the 1970s, when the city inaugurated its new subway system and the street was turned into one of Europe's first pedestrian-only zones. Take a moment to absorb the scene—you're standing in an area surrounded by history, postwar rebuilding, grand architecture, fine cafés, and people enjoying life…for me, quintessential Europe. (As you stroll down the Graben, refresh at the modern water dispenser.)

The street called Dorotheergasse, stretching to your left, leads to the **Dorotheum** auction house. Consider poking your nose in here later for some fancy window shopping (see page 128). Also along this street is the recommended sandwich shop Buffet Trześniewski—one of my favorite places for lunch.

In the middle of the Graben is the extravagantly blobby **⑫ Holy Trinity plague column** *(Pestsäule)*. The 60-foot pillar of clouds sprouts angels and cherubs, with the wonderfully gilded Father, Son, and Holy Ghost at the top (all protected by an anti-pigeon net).

In 1679, Vienna was hit by a massive epidemic of bubonic plague. Around 75,000 Viennese died—about a third of the city. Emperor Leopold I dropped to his knees (something emperors never did in public) and begged God to save the city. (Find Leopold about a quarter of the way up the monument, just above the brown banner. Hint: The typical inbreeding of royal families left him with a gaping underbite.) His prayer was heard by Lady Faith (the statue below Leopold, carrying a cross). With the help of a heartless little cupid, she tosses an old naked woman—symbolizing the plague—into the abyss and saves the city. In gratitude, Leopold vowed to erect this monument, which became a model for other cities ravaged by the same plague.

▶ *Thirty yards past the plague monument, look down the short street to the right, which frames a Baroque church with a stately green dome.*

⑬ St. Peter's Church

Leopold I ordered this church to be built as a thank-you for surviving the 1679 plague. The church stands on the site of a much older one that may have been Vienna's first (or second) Christian church. Inside, St. Peter's shows Vienna at its Baroque best (see page 128). Note that the church offers free organ concerts (advertised at the entry).

Graben with its gold-tipped plague column

The emperor prays for Vienna to be saved.

Adolf Loos (1870-1933)

"Decoration is a crime," wrote Adolf Loos, the turn-of-the-20th-century architect who was Vienna's answer to Frank Lloyd Wright. He lived in a time when most buildings were plastered with fake Greek columns, frosted with Baroque balustrades, and studded with statues. But Loos—foreshadowing the Modernist style of "less is more" and "form follows function"—stripped buildings down to their structural skeletons.

On this walk, you'll pass four Loos-designed structures. The **American Bar** (a half-block off Kärntner Strasse, on the left just before Stephansplatz at Kärntner Durchgang 10) has a cubical facade, with square columns and crossbeams (and no flowery capitals). The interior is elegant and understated, with rich marble and mirrors that appear to expand the small space. As the management has little patience with gawkers, the

best way to admire the interior is to sit down and order a cocktail. Farther ahead are Loos' **public WCs** (on Graben), the cube-shaped **Manz Bookstore** (Kohlmarkt 16), and the boldly stripped-down **Loos House** on Michaelerplatz.

▶ *Continue west on the Graben, where you'll immediately find some stairs leading underground to...*

⑭ Loos' Loos

In about 1900, a local chemical maker needed a publicity stunt to prove that his chemicals really got things clean. He purchased two wine cellars under the Graben and had them turned into classy WCs in the Modernist style (designed by Adolf Loos—see sidebar), complete with chandeliers and finely crafted mahogany. While the chandeliers are gone, the restrooms remain a relatively appealing place to do your business. Locals and tourists happily pay €0.50 for a quick visit.

▶ *The Graben dead-ends at the aristocratic supermarket Julius Meinl am Graben (see listing on page 160). From here, you could turn right into Vienna's "golden corner," with the city's finest shops. But we'll turn left. In the distance is the big green-and-gold dome of the Hofburg, where we'll head soon. The street leading up to the Hofburg is...*

⓯ Kohlmarkt

This is Vienna's most elegant and unaffordable shopping street, lined with Cartier, Armani, Gucci, Tiffany, and the emperor's palace at the end. Strolling Kohlmarkt, daydream about the edible window displays at ⓰ **Demel,** the ultimate Viennese chocolate shop (#14, daily 9:00-19:00). The room is filled with Art Nouveau boxes of Empress Sisi's choco-dreams come true: *Kandierte Veilchen* (candied violet petals), *Katzenzungen* (cats' tongues), and so on. The cakes here are moist (compared to the dry Sacher tortes). The enticing window displays change monthly, reflecting current happenings in Vienna. Wander inside. There's an impressive cancan of Vienna's most beloved cakes—displayed to tempt visitors into springing for the €10 cake-and-coffee deal (point to the cake you want). Farther in, you can see the bakery in action. Sit inside, with a view of the cakemaking, or outside, with the street action (upstairs is less crowded). Shops like this boast "K.u.K."—signifying that during the Habsburgs' heyday, it was patronized by the *König und Kaiser* (king and emperor—same guy). If you happen to be looking through Demel's window at exactly 19:01, just after closing, you can witness one of the great tragedies of modern Europe: the daily dumping of its unsold cakes.

Next to Demel, the **Manz Bookstore** has a Loos-designed facade.

▶ *Kohlmarkt ends at the square called...*

Kohlmarkt, a high-end shopping street

Royals ate Demel's cakes—and so can you.

⑰ Michaelerplatz

This square is dominated by the **Hofburg Palace.** Study the grand Neo-Baroque facade, dating from about 1900. The four heroic giants illustrate Hercules wrestling with his great challenges (Emperor Franz Josef, who commissioned the gate, felt he could relate).

In the center of this square, a scant bit of **Roman Vienna** lies exposed just below street level.

Spin Tour: Do a slow, clockwise pan to get your bearings, starting (over your left shoulder as you face the Hofburg) with **St. Michael's Church,** which offers fascinating tours of its crypt (see page 127). To the right of that is the fancy **Loden-Plankl shop,** with traditional Austrian formalwear, including dirndls. Farther to the right, across Augustinerstrasse, is the wing of the palace that houses the **Spanish Riding School** and its famous white Lipizzaner stallions. Farther down this street lies **Josefsplatz,** with the Augustinian Church (see page 124), and the Dorotheum auction house. At the end of the street are Albertinaplatz and the opera house (where we started this walk).

Continue your spin: Two buildings over from the Hofburg (to the right), the modern **Loos House** (now a bank) has a facade featuring a perfectly geometrical grid of square columns and windows. This was Vienna's first Modernist building (see sidebar). Compared to the ornate facade of the Hofburg, the stern Loos House appears to be from an entirely different age. And yet, both of these—as well as the Eiffel Tower and Mad Ludwig's fairy-tale Neuschwanstein Castle—were built in the same generation, roughly around 1900. In many ways, this jarring juxtaposition exemplifies the architectural turmoil of the turn of the 20th century, and represents the passing of the torch from Europe's age of divine monarchs to the modern era.

▶ *Let's take a look at where Austria's glorious history began—at the...*

Hofburg Imperial Palace

This is the complex of palaces where the Habsburg emperors lived out their lives (except in summer, when they resided at Schönbrunn Palace). Enter the Hofburg through the gate, where you immediately find yourself beneath a big rotunda. The doorway on the right is the entrance to the ⑱ **Imperial Apartments,** where the Habsburg emperors once lived in chandeliered elegance. Today you can tour its lavish rooms, a museum about Empress Sisi, and a porcelain and silver collection (✪ see the

Michaelerplatz: Where New Faces Down Old

It's fascinating to think of Michaelerplatz as the architectural embodiment of a fundamental showdown that took place at the dawn of the 20th century, between the old and the new.

Emperor Franz Josef came to power during the popular revolution year of 1848 (as an 18-year-old, he was locked in his palace for safety). Once in power, he saw that the real threat to him was not from without, but from within. He dismantled the city wall and moved his army's barracks to the center of the city. But near the end of his reign, the modern world was clearly closing in.

Franz Josef's Neo-Baroque design for the Hofburg, featuring huge statues of Hercules in action at the gate, represents a desperate last stand of the absolutism of the emperor. Hercules was a favorite of emperors— a prototype of the modern ruler. The only mythical figure that was half-god, Hercules earned this half-divinity with hard labor. Like Hercules, the emperor's position was a combination of privileged birth and achievement—legitimized both by God and by his own hard work.

A few decades after Franz Josef erected his celebration of divine right, Loos responded with his starkly different house across the street. Although the Loos House might seem ordinary, in its time, this anti-Historicist, anti-Art Nouveau statement was shocking. Inspired by his studies in the US (and by Frank Lloyd Wright), it was Vienna's first "modern" building, with a trapezoidal footprint that makes no attempt to hide the awkwardly shaped corner it stands on. Windows lack the customary cornice framing the top—a "house without eyebrows."

And so, from his front door, the emperor had to look at the modern world staring him rudely in the face, sneering, "Divine power is B.S. and your time is past." The emperor was angered by the bank building's lack of decor. Loos relented only slightly by putting up the 10 flower boxes (or "moustaches") beneath the windows.

But a few flowers couldn't disguise the notion that the divine monarchy was beginning to share Vienna with new ideas. As Loos worked, Stalin, Hitler, Trotsky, and Freud were all rattling about Vienna. Women were smoking and riding bikes. It was a scary time...a time ripe with change. And, of course, by 1918, after a Great War, the Habsburgs and the rest of Europe's imperial families were history.

Hofburg entrance in Neo-Rococo style

One of many courtyards in the vast palace

Hofburg Imperial Apartments Tour chapter). To the left is the ticket office for the ⑲ **Spanish Riding School** (see page 123).

Continuing on, you emerge from the rotunda into the main courtyard of the Hofburg, called **In der Burg.** The Caesar-like statue is of Habsburg Emperor Franz II (1768-1835), grandson of Maria Theresa, grandfather of Franz Josef, and father-in-law of Napoleon. To the right of Franz are the Imperial Apartments, and to the left are the offices of Austria's mostly-ceremonial president (the more powerful chancellor lives in a building just behind this courtyard).

Franz II faces a colorful red, black, and gold gateway that leads to the oldest part of the palace. This used to be a drawbridge over a moat, protecting the Hofburg's original fortress. Through the gate lies the ⑳ **Treasury** (Schatzkammer; ✪ see the Hofburg Treasury Tour chapter) and the **Imperial Music Chapel** (Hofmusikkapelle, see page 188), where—ever since Joseph Haydn and Franz Schubert were choirboys here—the famed Vienna Boys' Choir sings Mass.

▶ *Let's explore a bit more of the Hofburg. Facing the statue of Franz, turn left, passing through the tunnel, with a few tourist shops and restaurants, to spill out into...*

㉑ Heldenplatz (Heroes' Square)

In this spacious square of impressive buildings, statues, and views, you get a sense of the grand vision of the Habsburg rulers. On the left is the curved facade of the **New Palace** (Neue Burg). Built in the early 1900s, this was to have been the new Habsburg living quarters. But in 1914, the heir to the throne, Archduke Franz Ferdinand—while waiting politely for his long-lived uncle, Emperor Franz Josef, to die—was assassinated in Sarajevo. The

In Heldenplatz, a 20th-century extension of the Hofburg, a heroic statue gazes toward City Hall.

archduke's death sparked World War I and the eventual end of eight centuries of Habsburg rule. Today the building houses the **New Palace museums,** an eclectic collection of weaponry, armor, musical instruments, and ancient Greek statues (see page 122).

The two equestrian statues on the square depict Prince Eugene of Savoy (1663-1736), who battled the Ottoman Turks, and Archduke Charles (1771-1847), who battled Napoleon.

Imagine this huge square in 1938, when 300,000 Viennese gathered here to welcome Adolf Hitler and celebrate their annexation with Germany—the *"Anschluss."* The Nazi tyrant stood on the balcony of the New Palace and declared, "Before the face of German history, I declare my former homeland now a part of the Third Reich. One of the pearls of the Third Reich will be Vienna." He never said "Austria," a word that was now forbidden.

Many Austrians willingly accepted Hitler's rule. Remember, Austria—once a vast and mighty empire of 50 million—had emerged from World

Marie Theresa ruled Habsburg Austria for 40 years.

War I as a tiny, weak nation. Hitler promised jobs and a return to greatness—and the Austrian people gobbled it up.

Standing here, it's fascinating to consider Austrian aspirations for grandeur. In fact, the Habsburgs envisioned an ancient-Rome-inspired Imperial Forum stretching from here across the Ringstrasse.

Walk on through the Greek-columned passageway (the Äusseres Burgtor), cross the Ringstrasse, and stand between the giant Kunsthistorisches and Natural History museums—purpose-built in the 1880s to house the private art and scientific collections of the empire and to celebrate its culture and power. The emperor planned to tie these grand buildings and the palace together with two mighty triumphal arches spanning the Ringstrasse, connecting them into an awe-inspiring ensemble. While the emperor's vision died with his empire, a huge statue of perhaps the greatest of the Habsburgs, ㉒ **Maria Theresa,** stands in the center of it all.

▶ *You're in the heart of Viennese sightseeing. Surrounding this square are some of the city's top museums. And the Hofburg Palace itself contains many of Vienna's best sights and museums. From the opera to the Hofburg, from chocolate to churches, from St. Stephen's to Sacher tortes—Vienna waits for you.*

St. Stephen's Cathedral Tour

This massive church is the Gothic needle around which Vienna spins. According to the medieval vision of its creators, it stands like a giant jeweled reliquary, offering praise to God from the center of the city. The church and its towers, especially the 450-foot south tower, give the city its most iconic image. (Check your pockets for €0.10 coins; those minted in Austria feature the south tower on the back.) The cathedral has survived Vienna's many wars and today symbolizes the city's spirit and love of freedom.

The church has several worthwhile sights—some free, some requiring admission. On this tour, we'll pay to see the interior's main sights, and point out others you can see on your own.

The tower the locals call *Steffl* ("Stevie") still dominates the city as it did in this 19th-century watercolor.

ORIENTATION

Cost: It's free to enter the foyer and north aisle of the church, but it costs €4.50 to get into the main nave, where most of the interesting items are located (more for special exhibits). The south and north towers, catacombs, treasury, and audioguide cost extra. The €14 combo-ticket covers everything but is overkill for most visitors.

Hours: The church doors are open daily 6:00-22:00 (from 7:00 on Sun), but the main nave is open for tourists Mon-Sat 9:00-11:30 & 13:00-16:30, Sun 13:00-16:30, June-Aug until 18:30. During services, the main nave, north tower elevator, and catacombs close to tourists.

Information: Tel. 01/515-523-526, www.stephanskirche.at.

Tours: The €5.50 tours in English are entertaining (daily at 10:30, check info board inside entry to confirm schedule; price includes main nave entry, minimum 5 people). The €1 audioguide is helpful. ∩ Download my free St. Stephen's Cathedral audio tour.

Treasury: Tucked away in a loft in the oldest part of the church (accessed by an elevator just inside the cathedral's entry) is a collection of precious relics, dazzling church art, a portrait of Rudolf IV (considered the earliest German portrait), and views down on the nave (€5.50, includes audioguide, daily 9:00-16:30, July-Aug until 17:30).

Catacombs: Open only by guided tour (in German and English), meet in loft (north) transept, pay at the end (€5.50, daily generally on the half-hour, 10:00-11:30 & 13:30-16:30).

Towers: The iconic **south tower** offers great views and lots of stairs (€4.50, daily 9:00-17:30). The shorter **north tower** holds the famous "Pummerin" bell and is easier to ascend (elevator) but has lesser views (€5.50, daily 9:00-17:30 & 19:00-21:30).

English Mass: Each Saturday at 19:00.

Theft Alert: Inside and out, it's a favorite for pickpockets.

Starring: The cathedral's mighty exterior and evocative interior, including an ornately carved pulpit and various bits and pieces of Austrian history.

St. Stephen's Cathedral

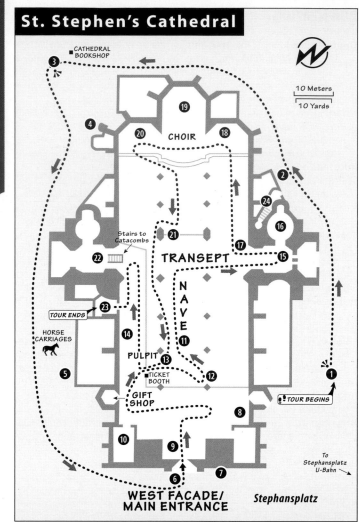

CATHEDRAL BOOKSHOP

10 Meters
10 Yards

3

4

19

20 CHOIR 18

2

24

16

Stairs to Catacombs

22

21

TRANSEPT

17

15

NAVE

23

TOUR ENDS

14

HORSE CARRIAGES

11

PULPIT

13

12

5

TICKET BOOTH

GIFT SHOP

8

10

9

6 7

WEST FACADE/ MAIN ENTRANCE

Stephansplatz

TOUR BEGINS

1

To Stephansplatz U-Bahn

St. Stephen's Cathedral

- ❶ South Side View & Old Photos
- ❷ Reliefs, Memorials & Former Tombstones
- ❸ North Tower View
- ❹ Pulpit with Vanquished Turk
- ❺ Stonemason's Hut
- ❻ West Facade & Main Entrance
- ❼ 05 Sign
- ❽ Maria Pócs Icon
- ❾ Organ & Treasury
- ❿ Chapel of Prince Eugene of Savoy
- ⓫ Main Nave
- ⓬ Pillar Statues (Madonna with the Protective Mantle)
- ⓭ Pulpit with Self-Portrait
- ⓮ Similar Self-Portrait
- ⓯ Mozart Plaque
- ⓰ Mozart Baptistery
- ⓱ Madonna of the Servants
- ⓲ Tomb of Frederick III
- ⓳ High Altar
- ⓴ Wiener Neustädter Altar
- ㉑ Plaque of Rebuilding
- ㉒ Catacombs Entry
- ㉓ North Tower (Elevator)
- ㉔ South Tower (Stairs)

THE TOUR BEGINS

Cathedral Exterior

Before we go inside, let's circle around the cathedral for a look at its impressive exterior. We'll stop at several points along the way to take it all in.

❶ South Side View

▶ *As you face the church's main entry, go to the right across the little square. From here, you can absorb the sheer magnitude of this massive church, with its skyscraping spire.*

The church we see today is the third one on this spot. It dates mainly from 1300 to 1450, when builders expanded on an earlier structure and added two huge towers at the end of each transept. When it was built, St. Stephen's—covering almost an acre of land—was a huge church for what was then just a modest town of 10,000. The ruler who built the church was competing with St. Vitus Cathedral, which was being built at the same time in Prague; he made sure that Vienna's grand church was bigger than Prague's. This helped convince the region's religious authorities that Vienna deserved a bishop, thus making St. Stephen's a "cathedral." Politically, this helped Vienna become a city to be reckoned with, and it soon replaced Prague as the seat of the Holy Roman Empire.

WWII bomb damage has been lovingly repaired.

Habsburg eagles roost on the tiled roof.

The impressive 450-foot **south tower**—capped with a golden orb and cross—took two generations to build (65 years) and was finished in 1433. The tower is a rarity among medieval churches in that it was completed before the Gothic style—and the age of faith—petered out.

Find the Turkish **cannonball** stuck in a buttress (above the low, green roof on the middle buttress, marked with the date *1683*)—a remnant of one of several Ottoman sieges of the city.

The half-size **north tower** (223 feet), around the other side of the church, was meant to be a matching steeple. But around 1500, it was abandoned mid-construction, when the money was needed to defend the country against the Ottomans rather than to build church towers.

The nave's sharply pitched **roof** stands 200 feet tall and is covered in 230,000 colorful ceramic tiles. The zigzag pattern on the south side is purely decorative, with no special symbolism.

The cathedral was heavily damaged at the end of World War II. Nearby are some **old photos** showing the destruction. In 1945, Vienna was caught in the chaos between the occupying Nazis and the approaching Soviets. Allied bombs sparked fires in nearby buildings, and the embers leapt to the cathedral rooftop. The original timbered Gothic roof burned, the cathedral's huge bell crashed to the ground, and the fire raged for two days. Civic pride prompted a financial outpouring, and the roof was rebuilt to its original splendor by 1952—doubly impressive considering the bombed-out state of the country at that time. Locals who contributed to the postwar reconstruction each had a chance to "own" one tile for their donation.

The little buildings lining the church exterior are **sacristies** (utility buildings used for running the church).

▶ *Circle the church exterior counterclockwise, passing the entrance to the south tower. If you're up for climbing the 343 stairs to the top, you could do it now, but it's better to wait until the end of this tour (tower climb described at the end of this chapter).*

Near the tower entrance, look for the carved ❷ **reliefs and memorials** and former **tombstones** now decorating the church wall. These are a reminder that the area around the church was a graveyard until 1780.

Look high above at the colorful **roof tiles,** with the double-headed **Habsburg eagle,** the date 1831, and the initials *FI* (for Austrian Emperor Franz I, who ruled when the roof was installed).

▶ *As you hook around behind the church, look for the cathedral bookshop (Dombuchhandlung) at the end of the block. Pause in front of that shop.*

❸ North Tower View

This spot provides a fine, wide-angle view of the stubby north tower and the apse of the church. From this vantage point, you can see the exoskeletal fundamentals of **Gothic architecture:** buttresses shoring up a very

The dome-capped north tower is smaller but has the big bell that rings in Austria's New Year.

heavy roof, allowing for large windows that could be filled with stained glass to bathe the interior in colorful light. A battalion of storm-drain gargoyles stands ready to vomit water during downpours. Colored tiles on the roof show not the two-headed eagle of Habsburg times (as on the other side), but two distinct eagles of modern times (1950): the state of Austria on the left and the city of Vienna on the right.

Just above street level, notice the marble ❹ **pulpit** under the golden starburst. The priest would stand here, stoking public opinion against the Ottomans, in front of crowds far bigger than could fit into the church. Above the pulpit (in a scene from around 1700), a saint stands victoriously atop a vanquished Turk.

▶ *Continue circling the church, passing a line of horse carriages waiting to take tourists for a ride. Watch for the blocky, modern-looking building huddled next to the side of the cathedral. This is the...*

❺ Stonemason's Hut

There's always been a stonemason's hut here, as workers must keep the church in good repair. Even today, the masonry is maintained in the traditional way—a never-ending task. Unfortunately, the local limestone used in the Middle Ages is quite porous and absorbs modern pollution. Until the 1960s, this was a very busy traffic circle, and today's acidic air still takes its toll. Each winter, when rainwater soaks into the surface and then freezes, the stone corrodes—and must be repaired. Your church entry ticket helps fund this ongoing work.

Across the street (past the horse carriages) is the **archbishop's palace,** where the head of this church still lives today (enjoying a very short commute).

▶ *Around the corner is the cathedral's front door. Stand at the back of the square, across from the main entrance, to take in the entire...*

❻ West Facade

The Romanesque-style main entrance is the oldest part of the church (c. 1240—part of a church that stood here before). Right behind you is the site of Vindobona, a Roman garrison town. Before the Romans converted to Christianity, there was a pagan temple here, and this entrance pays homage to that ancient heritage. Roman-era statues are embedded in the facade, and the two **octagonal towers** flanking the main doorway are dubbed the "heathen towers" because they're built with a few recycled

Horse carriages cluster at the cathedral.

"05"—symbol of anti-Nazi resistance

Roman stones (flipped over to hide the pagan inscriptions and expose the smooth sides).

Ten yards to the right of the main doorway, about chest high, is the symbol ❼ **"O5,"** carved into the wall by anti-Nazi rebels (behind the Plexiglas, under the first plaque). The story goes that Hitler—who'd actually grown up in Austria—spurned his roots. When he attained power, he refused to call the country "Österreich," its native name, insisting on the Nazi term "Ostmark." Austrian patriots wrote the code "O5" to keep the true name alive: The "5" stands for the fifth letter of the alphabet (E), which often stands in for an umlaut, giving the "O" its correct pronunciation for "Österreich."

Before entering, study the details of the **main doorway.** Christ—looking down from the tympanum over the door—is triumphant over death. Flanked by angels with dramatic wings, he welcomes all. Ornate, tree-like pillars support a canopy of foliage and creatures, all full of meaning to the faithful medieval worshipper. The fine circa-1240 carvings above the door were once brightly painted. The paint was scrubbed off in the 19th century, when pure stone was more in vogue.

▶ *Enter the church.*

Cathedral Foyer

Find a spot to peer through the gate down the immense nave—more than a football field long and nine stories tall. It's lined with clusters of slender pillars that soar upward to support the ribbed crisscross arches of the ceiling. Stylistically, the nave is Gothic with a Baroque overlay. It's a spacious, glorious venue that's often used for high-profile concerts (there's a ticket office back outside). We'll venture down the main nave soon, but first, take some time to explore the foyer area.

To the right as you enter, in a gold-and-silver sunburst frame, is a crude Byzantine-style ⑧ **Maria Pócs Icon** (Pötscher Madonna), brought here from a humble Hungarian village church. The picture of Mary and Child is said to have wept real tears in 1697, as Central Europe was once again being threatened by the Turks. Prince Eugene of Savoy (described later) saved the day at the Battle of Zenta in modern-day Serbia—a victory that broke the back of the Ottoman army. The crowds of pilgrims leaving flowers or lighting candles around the icon are most likely Hungarians thanking the Virgin for helping Prince Eugene drive the Ottomans out of their homeland.

Over the foyer's main doorway is the choir loft, with the 10,000-pipe ⑨ **organ,** a 1960 replacement for the famous one destroyed during World War II. This organ is also one of Europe's biggest, but it's currently broken and sits unused...too large to remove. Architects aren't sure whether it serves a structural purpose and adds support to the actual building.

Along the left wall is the **gift shop.** Step in to marvel at the 14th-century statuary decorating its wall—some of the finest carvings in the church.

The nave—a football field long and nine stories tall—has massive pillars sporting 77 statues.

To the left of the gift shop is the gated entrance to the ⑩ **Chapel of Prince Eugene of Savoy.** Prince Eugene (1663-1736), a teenage seminary student from France, arrived in Vienna in 1683 as the city was about to be overrun by the Ottoman Turks. He volunteered for the army and helped save the city, launching a brilliant career as a military man for the Habsburgs. His specialty was conquering the Ottomans. When he died, the grateful Austrians buried him here, under this chapel, marked by a tomb hatch in the floor.

▶ *Nearby is the entrance to the main nave. Buy a ticket and walk to the center.*

⑪ Main Nave

▶ *Looking down the nave, note the statues on the columns (about 30-40 feet above the ground).*

⑫ Pillar Statues

The nave's columns are richly populated with 77 life-size stone statues making a saintly parade to the high altar.

Check out the first pillar on the right. Facing the side wall is the **Madonna with the Protective Mantle,** shown giving refuge to people of all walks of life (notice all the happy people of faith tucked under her cape). Also on that same pillar, find Moses with the Ten Commandments (to the left of the Madonna, but hard to see because of the barrier). On other columns, Bible students can find their favorite characters and saints—more Madonnas, St. George (killing the dragon), St. Francis of Assisi, arrow-pierced St. Sebastian, and so on.

▶ *Start down the nave toward the altar. At the second pillar on the left is the*

⑬ Pulpit

The Gothic sandstone pulpit (c. 1500) is a masterpiece carved from three separate blocks (see if you can find the seams). A spiral stairway winds up to the lectern, surrounded and supported by the four church "fathers," whose writings influenced early Catholic dogma. Each has a very different and very human facial expression (from back to front): Ambrose (day-dreamer), Jerome (skeptic), Gregory (explainer), and Augustine (listener).

The pulpit is as crammed with religious meaning as it is with beautifully realistic carvings. The top of the stairway's railing swarms with lizards

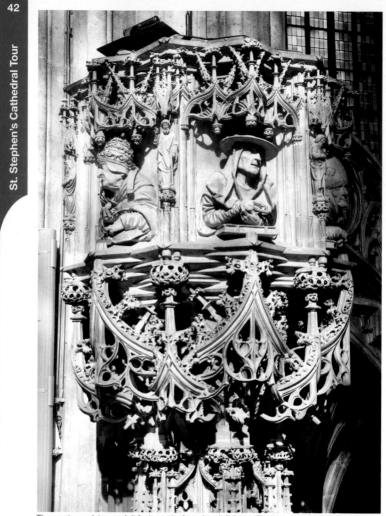

The ornate sandstone pulpit features the four church fathers. (That's Jerome in the hat.)

(animals of light) and toads (animals of darkness). The "Dog of the Lord" stands at the top, making sure none of those toads pollutes the sermon. Below the toads, wheels with three parts (the Trinity) roll up, while wheels with four spokes (the four seasons and four cardinal directions, symbolizing mortal life on earth) roll down.

Find the guy peeking out from under the stairs. This may be a **self-portrait** of the sculptor. In medieval times, art was done for the glory of God, and artists worked anonymously. But this pulpit was carved as humanist Renaissance ideals were creeping in from Italy—and individual artists were becoming famous. So the artist included what may be a rare self-portrait bust in his work. He leans out from a window, sculptor's compass in hand, to observe the world and his work. The artist's identity, however, is disputed. Long thought to be Hungarian mason Anton Pilgram, many scholars now believe it's Dutch sculptor Nicolaes Gerhaert van Leyden; both worked extensively on the cathedral.

About 20 paces toward the front, peering out from the left wall (about 15 feet up), is a similar ⑭ **self-portrait** of Pilgram (or is it Gerhaert?) in color, taken from the original organ case. He holds a compass and L-square and symbolically shoulders the heavy burden of being a master builder of this huge place.

▶ *Continue up the nave. We'll visit several sights at the front of the church, moving in a roughly counterclockwise direction.*

When you reach the gate that cuts off the front of the nave, turn right and enter the south transept. Go all the way to the doors, then look left to find the...

Even the pulpit's staircase is symbolic.

The sculptor is depicted nearby.

Mozart's Vienna

Wolfgang Amadeus Mozart (1756-1791) was married in St. Stephen's, attended Mass here, and had two of his children baptized here.

Mozart spent most of his adult life in Vienna. Born in Salzburg, Mozart was a child prodigy who toured Europe. He performed for Empress Maria Theresa's family in Vienna when he was eight. At 25, he left Salzburg in a huff (freeing himself from his domineering father) and settled in Vienna. Here he found instant fame as a concert pianist and freelance composer, writing *The Marriage of Figaro, Don Giovanni,* and *The Magic Flute.* He married Constanze Weber in St. Stephen's, and they set up house in a lavish apartment a block east of the church (now the lackluster Mozarthaus Vienna Museum—see page 129). Mozart lived at the heart of Viennese society—among musicians, actors, and aristocrats. He played in a string quartet with Joseph Haydn. At church, he would have heard Beethoven's teacher playing the organ.

After his early success, Mozart fell on hard times, and the couple had to move to the suburbs. When Mozart died at 35 (in 1791), he wasn't buried at St. Stephen's, because the cemetery that once surrounded the church had been cleared out a decade earlier as an anti-plague measure. Instead, his remains were dumped into a mass grave outside of town. But he was honored with a funeral service in St. Stephen's—held in the Prince Eugene of Savoy Chapel, where they played his famous (but unfinished) *Requiem.*

⑮ Mozart Chapel and Plaque

A plaque on the wall honors one of Vienna's most famous citizens—Wolfgang Amadeus Mozart, who had strong ties to this cathedral (see sidebar).

Look into the adjacent chapel at the fine ⑯ **baptistery** (stone bottom, matching carved-wood top, from around 1500). This is where Mozart's children were baptized.

On the right-hand column near the entrance to the south transept, notice the fine carved statue of the ⑰ **Madonna of the Servants** (from 1330). This remains a favorite of working people.

▶ *Now walk down the right aisle to the front. Dominating the chapel at the front right corner of the church is the...*

⑱ Tomb of Frederick III

This imposing, red-marble tomb is like a big king-size-bed coffin with an effigy of Frederick lying on top (not visible—but there's a photo of the effigy on the left). The top of the tomb is decorated with his coats of arms, representing the many territories he ruled over. It's likely by the same Nicolaes Gerhaert van Leyden who may have done the pulpit.

Frederick III (1415-1493) is considered the "father" of Vienna for turning the small village into a royal town with a cosmopolitan feel. Frederick secured a bishopric, turning the newly completed St. Stephen's church into a cathedral. The emperor's major contribution to Austria, however, was in fathering Maximilian I and marrying him off to Mary of Burgundy, instantly making the Habsburg Empire a major player in European politics. The lavish tomb (made of marble from Salzburg) is as long-lasting as Frederick's legacy. To make sure it stayed that way, locals saved the tomb from damage during World War II by encasing it in a shell of brick.

▶ *Walk to the middle of the church and face the...*

⑲ High Altar

The tall, ornate, black marble altarpiece (1641, by Tobias and Johann Pock) is topped with a statue of Mary that barely fits under the towering vaults of the ceiling. It frames a large painting of the stoning of St. Stephen, painted on copper. Stephen (at the bottom), having refused to stop professing his faith, is pelted with rocks by angry pagans. As he kneels, ready to die, he gazes up to see a vision of Christ, the cross, and the angels of heaven.

Tomb of Frederick III, Vienna's patron…

…who commissioned this altarpiece

The stained glass behind the painting—some of the oldest in the church—creates a kaleidoscopic jeweled backdrop.

▶ *Ten steps to the left of the main altar is the...*

⑳ Wiener Neustädter Altar

The triptych altarpiece—the symmetrical counterpart of Frederick III's tomb—was commissioned by Frederick in 1447. Its gilded wooden statues are especially impressive.

▶ *Walk back up the middle of the nave, toward the gate. When you reach the gate, look immediately to the right (on the third column—with the gate attached). About 10 feet above the ground is the...*

㉑ Plaque of Rebuilding

St. Stephen's is proud to be Austria's national church. The plaque explains in German how each region contributed to the rebuilding after World War II: *Die Glocke* (the bell) was financed by the state of Upper Austria. *Das Tor* (the entrance portal) was from Steiermark, the windows from Tirol, the pews from Vorarlberg, the floor from Lower Austria, and so on.

During World War II, many of the city's top art treasures were stowed safely in cellars and salt mines—hidden by both the Nazi occupiers (to protect against war damage) and by citizens (to protect against Nazi looters). The stained-glass windows behind the high altar were meticulously dismantled and packed away. The pulpit was encased, like the tomb of Frederick III, in a shell of brick. As the war was drawing to a close, it appeared St. Stephen's would escape major damage. But as the Nazis were fleeing, the bitter Nazi commander in charge of the city ordered that the church be destroyed. Fortunately, his underlings disobeyed. Unfortunately, the church accidentally caught fire during Allied bombing shortly thereafter, and the wooden roof collapsed onto the stone vaults of the ceiling. The Tupperware-colored glass on either side of the nave dates from the 1950s. Before the fire, the church was lit mostly with clear Baroque-era windows.

▶ *Head back toward the main entrance. Along the north side of the nave, you have two options: Tour the catacombs or ascend the north tower (both described next). Or you can head outside for the pulse-raising climb up the south tower.*

Other Cathedral Sights

▶ *Near the middle of the church, at the left/north transept, is the entrance to the...*

㉒ Catacombs

The catacombs (viewable by guided tour only) hold the bodies—or at least the innards—of 72 Habsburgs, including that of Rudolf IV, the man who began building the south tower. This is where Austria's rulers were

Finish your tour by climbing the south tower for views across the city to the Vienna Woods.

buried before the Kaisergruft was built (see page 125), and where later Habsburgs' entrails were entombed. The copper urns preserve the imperial organs in alcohol. I touched Maria Theresa's urn and it wobbled.

▶ *Also in the north nave, but closer to the cathedral's main door, is the entrance for the north tower (look for the* Aufzug zur Pummerin *sign).*

㉓ North Tower

The cramped north tower elevator takes you to a mediocre view and a big bell. Nicknamed "the Boomer" (Pummerin), it's old (first cast in 1711), big (nearly 10 feet across), and very heavy (21 tons). By comparison, the Liberty Bell is four feet across and weighs one ton. The Pummerin was cast from cannons (and cannonballs) captured from the Ottomans when the siege of Vienna was lifted. These days, locals know the Pummerin as the bell that rings in the Austrian New Year.

▶ *Exit the church. Make a U-turn to the left if you're up for a climb up the...*

㉔ South Tower

The 450-foot-high tower, once key to the city's defense as a lookout point, is dear to Viennese hearts. (It's affectionately nicknamed "Steffl," Viennese for "Stevie.") No church spire in (what was) the Austro-Hungarian Empire is taller—by Habsburg decree. It offers a far better view than the north tower, but you'll earn it by hiking 343 tightly wound steps up the spiral staircase (this hike burns about one Sacher torte's worth of calories).

From the top, use your city map to locate the famous sights. There are great views of the colorful church roof, the low-level Viennese skyline (major skyscrapers are regulated in the city center), and—in the distance— the Vienna Woods.

▶ *Your tour is over. You're at the very center of Vienna. Explore.*

Ringstrasse Tram Tour

In the 1860s, Emperor Franz Josef had the city's medieval wall torn down
and replaced with a grand boulevard—the Ringstrasse—190 feet wide,
arcing three miles around the city's core, and lined with grand buildings.

This self-guided tram tour gives you a fun orientation and a ridicu-
lously quick glimpse of some of the Ringstrasse's great sights as you glide
by. Vienna's trams—that is, streetcars—are sleek and modern. The system
is easy to master. This 45-minute tour starts and ends at the same convenient place, the centrally located opera house. Along the way, we'll see
Vienna in all its turn-of-the-century glory. There's the grand Ring road itself,
with its classy buildings and pleasant parks. You'll see sights and museums you may want to visit later. And we'll make a stop midway through to
see the not-so-blue Danube. It's a no-stress way to enjoy Vienna as you sit
shoulder-to-shoulder with ordinary Viennese.

ORIENTATION

Cost: €2.20 (one transit ticket), €2.30 if bought from coin-op machine on tram. A single ticket can be used to cover the whole route, including the transfer between trams (but you're not otherwise allowed to interrupt your trip). With a transit pass, you're free to hop off, sightsee, then hop back on another tram (they come along every few minutes). For more on riding Vienna's trams, see page 174.

When to Go: It's pleasant by day or night (when nearly every sight is well-lit).

Pricier Option: A yellow just-for-tourists streetcar circles the Ring without requiring a transfer—but it costs more and runs less frequently (€9 for one 30-minute loop, 2/hour 10:00-17:30, see page 190).

Bike Option: Renting a bike (see page 175) allows you to easily stop at sights or to detour to nearby points of interest. The grassy median strip has excellent bike paths that run along almost the entire circuit of the Ring (except for a few blocks after the votive church, near the end of this tour).

Tours: ⌒ Download my free Ringstrasse Tram audio tour.

Length of This Tour: About 45 minutes; allow more time if you hop off along the way.

Starring: Vienna's grandest boulevard, major landmarks, and a dizzyingly quick, once-over-lightly look at the city.

The Oper stop, where we catch our tram.

Our Ringstrasse tour uses trams #1 and #2.

THE TOUR BEGINS

▶ *Start at the Oper tram stop, in the middle of the Ringstrasse, in front of the opera house. To get there from the opera house, take the underpass, following signs with the tram symbol to Opernring. As you emerge back on street level, the Oper tram stop is to your right.*

You want **Tram #2** *going counterclockwise around the Ring—that is, the one marked Friedrich-Engels-Platz. (It's the one going against the direction of car traffic.) Before boarding, read the following to plan your trip.*

Riding the Tram

To make our circular route, we'll need to take two different trams, with a transfer in between. First, we'll take Tram #2. At the Danube (the stop called Schwedenplatz), we'll get off and transfer to Tram #1 to complete the loop. Trams come along every 5 or 10 minutes.

A single ticket covers the entire trip, including the transfer. You can buy it directly from the driver. A transit pass (like the good-value 24-hour pass) works even better, allowing you to hop on and off to sightsee as you like. Some of the best stops are: Weihburggasse (the greenery of Stadtpark), Rathausplatz (City Hall and its summertime food circus), and Burgring (Kunsthistorisches Museum and Hofburg Palace).

This tour lists each tram stop you'll pass, and tells you which way to look along the way. Stop names are announced in German as you approach and labeled (in small, sometimes hard-to-read lettering) at the stops themselves. Be aware that if no one requests a particular stop, the tram may zip on through.

You'll find that the tram goes faster than you can read. It's best to look through this chapter ahead of time, then ride with an eye out for the various sights described here.

▶ *Let's go. Board Tram #2, and, if you can, grab a seat on the right-hand side, with a clear view out. Before you leave the* **Oper stop...**

❶ Look Left

Just next to the opera house, the city's main pedestrian drag, Kärntner Strasse, leads to the zigzag-mosaic roof of **St. Stephen's Cathedral.** This tram tour makes a 360-degree circle around the cathedral, staying

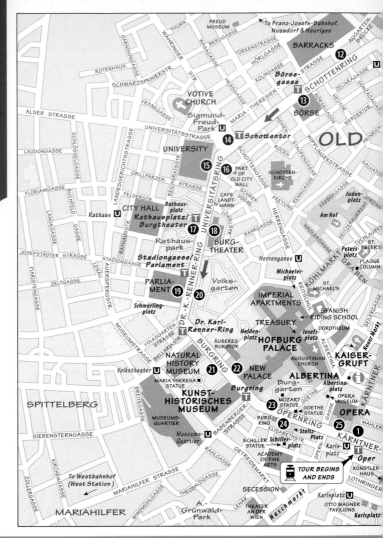

Ringstrasse Tram Tour

Note: Numerals on this map indicate points of interest described in this chapter.

Schottenring

Tabor-strasse

To Prater

Praterstern Wien Nord

FRANZ-JOSEFS-KAI

Danube Canal

Salztor-brücke

MON. TO GESTAPO VICTIMS

Dock for Twin City Liner to Bratislava

CHANGE TRAMS

Morzin-platz

Schweden-platz

Nestroy-platz

Schwedenplatz

Julius-Raab-Platz

ST. RUPRECHT'S

LISSALON AM SCHWEDENPLATZ (ICE CREAM)

FRANZ - JOSEFS - KAI

URANIA BUILDING

To Kunsthaus Wien

Hoher Markt

TOWN

Julius-Raab-Platz

POSTAL SAVINGS BANK

FORMER MINISTRY OF WAR

ST. STEPHEN'S CATHEDRAL MUSEUM

Stephans-platz

DR. KARL LUEGER STATUE

STUBENRING

Dr.-Karl-Lueger-Platz

MAK

WIEN MITTE BAHNHOF

To Hundertwasser Haus

MOZART-HAUS

Stubentor

Landstrasse Wien Mitte

Franziskaner-platz

Stadtpark

PARKRING

Wien River

HAUS DER MUSIK

STRAUSS STATUE

SCHUBERT-RING

Stadtpark

Schwarzen-bergplatz

HOTEL IMPERIAL

EQUEST. STATUE

MUSIK-VEREIN

KONZERT-HAUS

WIEN MUSEUM

To Russian Monument, Belvedere Palace & Hauptbahnhof (Main Station)

Rochusgasse

250 Meters

250 Yards

A glimpse of the Russian monument

Stadtpark, one of Vienna's green spaces

about this same distance from the great church that marks the center of Vienna.

▶ *Seconds later...*

❷ Look Right

Along this stretch, you'll pass a string of Vienna's finest five-star hotels, including **Hotel Imperial**—the choice of nearly every visiting big shot, from the Rolling Stones to Queen Elizabeth.

Fifty yards after the hotel (also on the right), at Schwarzenbergplatz, an **equestrian statue** honors Prince Charles Schwarzenberg, who fought Napoleon. From the end of World War II until 1955, Austria and its capital were occupied by foreign troops, including Russian forces; during that time the square was named Stalinplatz after the Soviet dictator.

In the distance beyond the prince, at the far end of the long square, look for a fountain with a big colonnade just behind it. This **Russian monument** was built in 1945 as a forced thank-you to the Soviets for liberating Austria from the Nazis. Formerly a sore point, now the monument is just ignored.

▶ *Coming up soon is the **Schwarzenbergplatz stop**. When you pass it...*

❸ Look Right

Three blocks beyond the Schwarzenbergplatz stop is the huge **Stadtpark** (City Park). This inviting green space honors many great Viennese musicians and composers with statues. At the beginning of the park, the gold-and-cream concert hall behind the trees is the **Kursalon,** opened in 1867 by the Strauss brothers, who directed many waltzes here. Touristy Strauss concerts are held in this building (for details, see page 186). If the weather's nice, hop off at the next stop (Weihburggasse) for a stroll in the park.

▶ Right at the **Weihburggasse stop...**

❹ Look Right

In the park, barely visible from the tram (squint through the park gate a few yards beyond the stop), the gilded statue of "Waltz King" **Johann Strauss** holds a violin as he did when he conducted his orchestra, whipping his fans into a three-quarter-time frenzy.

▶ *The next four sights pass quickly, so read about them while you're waiting at the next stop* **(Stubentor).** *Just after the tram sets off again...*

❺ Look Left

Centered in a public square, is a bronze statue (now turned green) of **Dr. Karl Lueger,** the mayor who shaped Vienna into a modern city (see sidebar on page 62).

▶ *Immediately after the Lueger statue...*

Johann Strauss gets a statue in Stadtpark, near the Kursalon where his waltzes still play.

Hey, MAK! Here's a nice museum.

The Postal Savings Bank, by Otto Wagner

❻ Look Right

The big, red-brick building across the street is the **Museum of Applied Art** (MAK), showing furniture and design through the ages (also has good café and gift shop).

▶ *A block after the museum...*

❼ Look Right

The long, white building used to be the **Austrian Ministry of War**—back when that was a major operation. Above its oval windows, you can see busts of soldiers wearing Stratego-style military helmets. The equestrian statue at the entrance is Field Marshal Radetzky, a military big shot in the 19th century under Franz Josef.

▶ *Now (quickly or it's gone)...*

❽ Look Left

Radetzky is pointing across the street toward the **Postal Savings Bank** (set back on a little square). Designed by Otto Wagner, it's one of the rare Secessionist buildings facing the Ring. (For more on the Secession, see the sidebar on page 136.)

▶ *Immediately after the **Julius-Raab-Platz stop,** the tram makes a sharp left turn, when you should...*

❾ Look Right

The white-domed building on your right is the **Urania,** Franz Josef's 1910 observatory. On the horizon behind the Urania, visually trace the canal and squint to get a glimpse of the huge red cars of the giant hundred-year-old

The domed Urania, part of the parade of architectural styles on the Ring from circa 1900

Ferris wheel in Vienna's **Prater amusement park** (fun and characteristically Viennese, described on page 139).

▶ At the next stop, **Schwedenplatz...**

⑩ Get Off and Transfer

Hop off tram #2 at the Schwedenplatz stop and wait for tram #1 (heading in the same direction you've been going, and leaving from the next track, just to your left; trams come along every 5-10 minutes). Gelato fans may want to prolong the wait a little with a break at Eissalon am Schwedenplatz. Before venturing away, check the electronic board to see how many minutes you'll wait until the next tram arrives.

Notice the waterway next to you, and how blue it isn't. It's the Danube, specifically, the **Danube Canal**—a.k.a. the "Baby Danube." This is one of the many small arms of the Danube River. Modern engineering has channeled the rest of the river into a mightier stream farther away.

From the Black Forest in Germany, all the way to the Black Sea in Romania, the Danube flows 1,770 miles through 10 countries. It's Western Europe's longest river—twice as long as the Rhine. It's also the only major

While you wait between trams for Part II of our tour, enjoy a placid branch of the mighty Danube.

river flowing west to east, making it invaluable for commercial transportation. The Danube was, of course, immortalized by Johann Strauss, Jr.'s *The Blue Danube* waltz.

This southern bank was once the original Roman town, called Vindobona. Back then, the Danube marked the northern border of civilization itself. Venturing beyond the Danube put you in the Germanic land of the barbarians.

The Danube flows eastward through upper Austria. It's at its romantic best just upstream from Vienna, to the west. There it's lined with ruined castles, small towns, vineyards, and the glorious Melk Abbey. The modern boat station you see from here is where fast boats depart heading east to Bratislava—Slovakia's capital—just 90 minutes downstream.

Now look across the Danube Canal. If some of the buildings across the canal seem a bit drab, it's because this neighborhood was thoroughly bombed in World War II. These postwar buildings were constructed in the 1950s, on the cheap. Now, in a much more prosperous era, they're being replaced by sleek, futuristic buildings. They include the OPEC headquarters, where oil ministers often meet to set prices.

By the way, this is called Schwedenplatz ("Sweden Square") because after World War I, Vienna was overwhelmed with hungry orphans. The

Swedes took several thousand in, raised them, and finally sent them home healthy and well-fed.

▸ *Get ready—here comes tram #1. This time, grab a seat on the left if you can. Keep an eye toward the old city center. After three blocks, opposite the gas station (be ready—it passes fast)...*

⓫ Look Left

You'll see the ivy-covered walls and round Romanesque arches of **St. Ruprecht's** (Ruprechtskirche), the oldest church in Vienna. It was built in the 11th century on a bit of Roman ruins.

The low-profile, modern-looking, concrete **monument** in the corner of the park (close to the tram, on the left) commemorates the victims of the Gestapo, whose Austrian headquarters were here.

▸ *Take a breather for a bit—there's not much to see until after the next two stops (**Salztorbrücke** and **Schottenring**).*

In the Meantime...

Remember that the Ringstrasse replaced the mighty walls that once protected Vienna from external enemies.

Imagine the great imperial capital contained within its three-mile-long wall, most of which dated from the 16th to 18th century. As was typical of city walls, it was lined with cannons (2,200, in Vienna's case) and surrounded by a "shooting field" or "cannonball zone." This swath of land, as wide as a cannonball could fly (about 400 yards), was clear cut so no one could approach without being targeted.

After the popular unrest and uprisings of 1848, the emperor realized the true threat against him was from inside. He rid the city of its walls in about 1860, built this boulevard and transportation infrastructure (useful for moving citizens in good times and soldiers in bad), and, as you'll see in a moment, moved his army closer at hand. Napoleon III's remodel of Paris demonstrated that wide boulevards make it impossible for revolutionaries to erect barricades to block the movement of people and supplies. That encouraged Franz Josef to implement a similarly broad street plan for his Ring. A straight stretch of boulevard may seem just stately, but for an embattled emperor, it's an easy-to-defend corridor.

When the emperor had the walls taken down, the shooting field was wide open and ripe for development. Hence, the wonderful architecture that lines the outer edge of the Ringstrasse is all from the same era (post 1860).

▶ *The tram leaves the canal after the **Schottenring stop** and turns left. About 100 yards after that left turn, you should...*

⓬ Look Right

Through a gap in the buildings, you'll get a glimpse of a huge, red-brick castle—actually high-profile **barracks** built here at the command of a nervous Emperor Franz Josef (who found himself on the throne as an 18-year-old in 1848, the same year people's revolts against autocracy were sweeping across Europe).

▶ *When you pull into the **Börsegasse stop...***

⓭ Look Left

The orange-and-white, Neo-Renaissance temple of money—the **Börse**—is Vienna's stock exchange. The next block is lined with banks and insurance companies—the financial district of Austria.

▶ *At the next stop **(Schottentor)...***

⓮ Look Right

The huge, frilly, Neo-Gothic church across the small park is a **"votive church,"** a type of church built to fulfill a vow in thanks for God's help—in this case, when an 1853 assassination attempt on Emperor Franz Josef failed.

Also at the Schottentor stop, look ahead and left down the long, straight stretch of boulevard and imagine the city's impressive wall and that vast swath of no-man's land that extended from the former city wall as far as a cannonball could fly.

▶ *Just after the **Schottentor stop...***

⓯ Look Right

You're looking at the main building of the **University of Vienna** (Universität Wien). Established in 1365, the university has no real campus, as its buildings are scattered around town. It's considered the oldest continuously operating university in the German-speaking world.

▶ *Immediately opposite the university...*

⓰ Look Left

A chunk of the old **city wall** is visible (behind a gilded angel). Beethoven lived and composed in the building just above the piece of wall.

▶ *As you pull into the **Rathausplatz/Burgtheater stop,** first...*

The City Hall, with its Neo-Gothic spires, hosts a summer evening "scene" of food and music.

⑰ Look Right

The Neo-Gothic **City Hall** (Rathaus) flies both the flag of Austria and the flag of Europe. The square in front (Rathausplatz) is a festive site in summer, with a thriving food circus and a huge screen showing outdoor movies, operas, and concerts (mid-July-mid-Sept 11:00-late; see page 189). In December, City Hall becomes a huge Advent calendar, with 24 windows opening—one each day—as Christmas approaches.

▶ *And then...*

⑱ Look Left

Immediately across the street from City Hall is the **Burgtheater,** Austria's national theater. Locals brag it's the "leading theater in the German-speaking world." Next door (to the left of the theater—behind you now) is **Café Landtmann** (one of the city's finest, which opened for business even as the Burgtheater was being built).

▶ *Just after the **Stadiongasse/Parlament stop...***

The Birth of Modern Vienna

As Vienna's population grew in the 1800s from 500,000 to more than 2 million, the city needed to expand. The old medieval wall was torn down to create the Ringstrasse. The street was lined with leafy parks and Vienna's most important buildings—City Hall, Parliament, stock exchange, the ritziest cafés, the theater, art museum, and opera house. Back then, gas lamps lit the night, and horse-drawn trams clip-clopped under the trees. Buildings were state-of-the-art, but decorated in styles that echoed the past (often called "Historicism"). Some were Neoclassical—with Greek columns and Roman arches; others were Neo-Gothic, with the look of a medieval church, and so on.

Besides the Ring, the rest of Vienna was transformed in the late 1800s. The old water system of Roman-style aqueducts was replaced with modern plumbing. Thomas Edison was hired to install electric lights at Schönbrunn Palace. The Danube was tamed with flood controls. Engineers even began an artificial island that eventually became Danube Island.

Vienna's incredible transformation was overseen by three people: Emperor Franz Josef (who ruled for 68 years during Vienna's Golden Age), Mayor Karl Lueger, and chief architect Otto Wagner. In a few short decades, they turned the Ringstrasse—and Vienna—into the wonder of Europe.

⑲ Look Right

The Neo-Greek temple of democracy houses the **Austrian Parliament.** The lady with the golden helmet is Athena, goddess of wisdom.

▶ *And then swivel to...*

⑳ Look Left

Across the street from the Parliament is the imperial park called the **Volksgarten,** with a fine public rose garden.

▶ *The next stop is Dr. Karl-Renner-Ring. When the tram pulls away...*

㉑ Look Right

The vast building is the **Natural History Museum** (Naturhistorisches

Museum), which faces its twin, the **Kunsthistorisches Museum,** containing the city's greatest collection of paintings. The **MuseumsQuartier** behind them completes the ensemble with a collection of modern art museums. A hefty statue of Empress Maria Theresa squats between the museums, facing the grand gate to the Hofburg Palace.

▶ *Now...*

㉒ Look Left

Opposite Maria Theresa, the arched gate (the Äusseres Burgtor, the only surviving castle gate of the old town wall) leads to the **Hofburg,** the emperor's palace. Of the five arches, the center one was used only by the emperor.

Your tour is nearly finished, so consider hopping off here to visit the Hofburg, the Kunsthistorisches Museum, or one of the museums in the MuseumsQuartier.

▶ *Fifty yards after **the Burgring stop...***

㉓ Look Left

Until 1918, the appealing **Burggarten** was the private garden of the emperor. Today locals enjoy relaxing here, and it's also home to a famous statue of **Mozart** (hard to see from the tram).

On the right is the Burg Kino theater, which plays the movie *The Third Man* several times a week in English (see page 189).

A hundred yards farther (back on the left, just after the park), the German philosopher **Goethe** sits in a big, thought-provoking chair.

▶ *Now it's time to...*

The Burgtheater, still a working theater   Parliament, with its statue of Athena

㉔ Look Right

Goethe seems to be playing trivia with German poet **Schiller** across the street (in the little park set back from the street). Behind the statue of Schiller is the **Academy of Fine Arts** (described on page 131).

▶ Get ready to...

㉕ Look Left...and Get Off

Hey, there's the **opera house** again. Jump off the tram and see the rest of the city. (To join me on a walking tour of Vienna's center, which starts here at the opera; ✪ see the Vienna City Walk chapter.)

Tour over. Yes it's been a blur of passing sights, but it's also a good sightseeing overview.

Hofburg Imperial Apartments Tour

In this tour of the Hofburg Imperial Apartments, you'll see the lavish rooms that were home to the hardworking Emperor Franz Josef and his eccentric empress, "Sisi." From here, the Habsburgs ruled their vast empire.

Franz Josef was (for all intents and purposes) the last of the Habsburg monarchs, and these apartments straddle the transition from old to new. You'll see chandeliered luxury alongside office furniture and electric lights.

Franz Josef and Sisi were also a study in contrasts: Franz was earnest, practical, and spartan; Sisi was poetic, high-strung, and luxury-loving. Together, they lived in the cocoon of the Imperial Apartments, oblivious to how the world was changing around them.

The Hofburg, home of emperors for 600 years, and now the office of the Austrian president

ORIENTATION

Cost: €13, includes well-done audioguide; also covered by €29 Sisi Ticket (see page 180), which includes the Schönbrunn Palace Grand Tour and the Imperial Furniture Collection.

Hours: Daily 9:00-17:30, July-Aug until 18:00, last entry one hour before closing.

Information: Tel. 01/533-7570, www.hofburg-wien.at.

When to Go: It can be crowded mid-morning, so go either right at opening time or after 14:00.

Getting There: Enter from under the rotunda just off Michaelerplatz, through the Michaelertor gate.

Tours: The included audioguide brings the exhibits to life.

Length of This Tour: If you listen to the entire audioguide, allow nearly 2 hours: 40 minutes for the porcelain and silver collection, 30 minutes for the Sisi Museum, and 40 minutes for the apartments.

THE TOUR BEGINS

The Imperial Apartments are part of the large Hofburg Palace complex. Your ticket grants you admission to three separate exhibits, which you'll visit on a pretty straightforward one-way route. The first floor holds a collection of precious porcelain and silver knickknacks *(Silberkammer)*. You then go upstairs to the Sisi Museum, which has displays about her life. This leads into the 20 or so rooms of the Imperial Apartments *(Kaiserappartements),* starting in Franz Josef's rooms, then heading into the dozen rooms where his wife Sisi lived.

Imperial Porcelain and Silver Collection
▶ *Your visit (and the excellent audioguide) starts on the ground floor.*

Tableware Collection
The audioguide actually manages to make the Habsburg court's vast tableware collection fairly interesting. The cabinets are full (with the contents intact—this area was never bombed), and the displays were functional so that servants could select the proper items, as the royals would entertain up to 800 guests at a time. Browse the collection to gawk at the opulence and to take in some colorful Habsburg trivia. (Who'd have thunk that the

Hofburg Imperial Apartments Tour

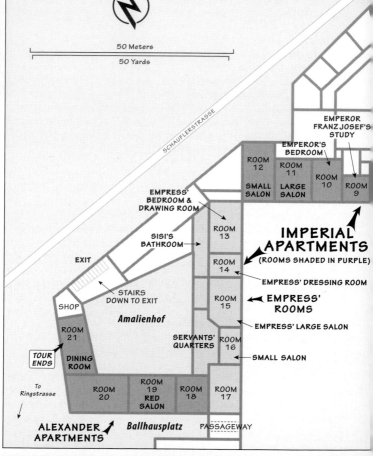

50 Meters

50 Yards

SCHAUFLERSTRASSE

EMPEROR FRANZ JOSEF'S STUDY

EMPEROR'S BEDROOM

ROOM 12

ROOM 11

ROOM 10

ROOM 9

SMALL SALON

LARGE SALON

EMPRESS' BEDROOM & DRAWING ROOM

ROOM 13

SISI'S BATHROOM

IMPERIAL APARTMENTS
(ROOMS SHADED IN PURPLE)

EXIT

ROOM 14

EMPRESS' DRESSING ROOM

STAIRS DOWN TO EXIT

EMPRESS' ROOMS

ROOM 15

SHOP

Amalienhof

EMPRESS' LARGE SALON

ROOM 21

SERVANTS' QUARTERS

ROOM 16

SMALL SALON

TOUR ENDS

DINING ROOM

To Ringstrasse

ROOM 20

ROOM 19 RED SALON

ROOM 18

ROOM 17

ALEXANDER APARTMENTS

Ballhausplatz

PASSAGEWAY

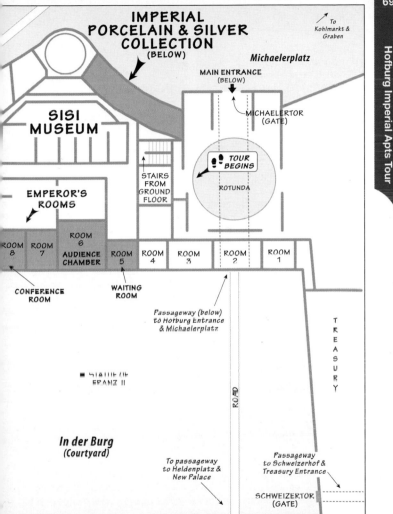

IMPERIAL
PORCELAIN & SILVER
COLLECTION
(BELOW)

To
Kohlmarkt &
Graben

Michaelerplatz

MAIN ENTRANCE
(BELOW)

MICHAELERTOR
(GATE)

SISI
MUSEUM

TOUR
BEGINS

STAIRS
FROM
GROUND
FLOOR

ROTUNDA

EMPEROR'S
ROOMS

ROOM
8

ROOM
7

ROOM
6
AUDIENCE
CHAMBER

ROOM
5

ROOM
4

ROOM
3

ROOM
2

ROOM
1

CONFERENCE
ROOM

WAITING
ROOM

Passageway (below)
to Hotburg Entrance
& Michaelerplatz

T
R
E
A
S
U
R
Y

STATUE OF
FRANZ II

ROAD

In der Burg
(Courtyard)

To passageway
to Heldenplatz &
New Palace

Passageway
to Schweizerhof &
Treasury Entrance

SCHWEIZERTOR
(GATE)

The visit begins with imperial porcelain.

The (included) audioguide is worthwhile.

court had an official way to fold a napkin—and that the technique remains a closely guarded secret?) Still, I wouldn't bog down here, as there's much more to see upstairs.

▶ Climb the stairs—the same staircase used by the emperors and empresses who lived here. At the top is a timeline of Sisi's life. Swipe your ticket to pass through the turnstile, consider the (rare) WC, and enter the room with the...

Model of the Hofburg

Circle to the far side to find where you're standing right now, near the smallest of the Hofburg's three domes. That small dome tops the entrance to the Hofburg from Michaelerplatz.

The Hofburg was the epicenter of one of Europe's great political powers—600 years of Habsburgs lived here. The Hofburg started as a 13th-century medieval castle (near where you are right now) and expanded over the centuries to today's 240,000-square-meter (60-acre) complex, now owned by the state.

To the left of the dome (as you face the facade) is the steeple of the Augustinian Church. It was there, in 1854, that Franz Josef married 16-year-old Elisabeth of Bavaria, and their story began.

▶ Now enter a darkened room at the beginning of the...

Sisi Museum

Empress Elisabeth (1837-1898)—a.k.a. "Sisi" (SEE-see)—was Franz Josef's mysterious, beautiful, and narcissistic wife. This museum traces her fabulous but tragic life with the help of her flowery poetry, which is posted for reading as you stroll through these ornate halls.

Sisi

Empress Elizabeth, known as Sisi since childhood, became an instant celebrity when she married Franz Josef at 16. Franz Josef was intended to marry Sisi's sister, but he chose Sisi instead—for love.

Sisi's main goals in life seem to have been preserving her reputation as a beautiful empress, maintaining her Barbie-doll figure, and tending to her fairy-tale, ankle-length hair. But, despite severe dieting and fanatical exercise, age took its toll. After turning 30, she refused to allow photographs or portraits, and was generally seen in public with a delicate fan covering her face (and bad teeth).

Politically, Sisi's personal cause was promoting Hungarian independence. Her personal tragedy was the death of her son Rudolf, the crown prince, in an apparent suicide (an incident often dramatized as the "Mayerling Affair"). Disliking Vienna and the confines of the court, Sisi traveled more and more frequently. As the years passed, the restless Sisi and her hardworking husband became estranged. In 1898, while visiting Geneva, Switzerland, she was murdered by an Italian anarchist.

Sisi's Death

The exhibit starts with Sisi's sad end, showing her **death mask**, photos of her **funeral procession** (by the Hercules statues facing Michaelerplatz), and an **engraving** of a grieving Franz Josef. It was at her death that the obscure, private empress' legend began to grow.

▶ Continue into the corridor.

The Sisi Myth

Newspaper clippings of the day make it clear that the empress was not a major public figure in her lifetime. She was often absent from public functions, and the censored press was gagged from reporting on her eccentricities. After her death, however, her image quickly became a commodity

The Sisi Museum introduces you to this exotic anorexic; then you tour her living quarters.

and began appearing on everyday items such as **candy tins** and **beer steins.**

The plaster-cast **statue** captures the one element of her persona everyone knew: her beauty. Sisi was nearly 5'8" (a head taller than her husband), had a 20-inch waist (she wore very tight corsets), and weighed only about 100 pounds. (Her waistline eventually grew...to 21 inches. That was at age 50, after giving birth to four children.) This statue, a copy of one of 30 statues that were erected in her honor in European cities, shows her holding one of her trademark fans. It doesn't show off her magnificent hair, however, which reached down as far as her ankles in her youth.

Sisi-mania really got going in the 1950s with a series of **movies** based on her life (starring Romy Schneider), depicting the empress as beautiful and innocent, and either crying or singing at any given point in the film.

▶ *Round the corner into the next room.*

Sisi's Childhood

Sisi grew up on a country estate in Bavaria, amid horses and woods, far from sophisticated city life. (See her **baby shoes** in a box and the picture of her **childhood palace.**) Franz Josef—who'd been engaged to her older sister—spied seemingly happy-go-lucky Sisi when she was 15 and fell in love. They married. At the wedding reception, Sisi burst into tears, the first sign that something was not right.

The Ballroom: Sisi at Court

In the glass display cases are replicas of her **gowns.** Big **portraits** of Sisi (considered the most realistic in existence) and Franz Josef show them dressed to the nines. **Jewels** (also replicas) reproduce some of the finery she wore as empress—but to her, they were her "chains." She hated official court duties and the constraints of public life, and hated being the center of attention. Sisi's mother-in-law dominated her child-rearing, her first-born died, and she complained that she couldn't sleep or eat. However, she did participate in one political cause—championing rights for Habsburg-controlled Hungary (see her **bust** and **portrait** as Queen of Hungary). She spoke Hungarian enthusiastically.

▶ *Head into the next, darkened room.*

Sisi's Beauty

Sisi longed for the carefree days of her youth. She began to withdraw from public life, passing time riding horses (see **horse** statuettes and pictures) and tending obsessively to maintaining her physical beauty. In the glass case on the right wall, you'll see some of her **menus,** and a **bill from Demel.** Her **recipes** for beauty preparations included creams and lotions as well as wearing a raw-meat face mask while she slept. Sisi weighed herself obsessively on her gold-trimmed **scale** and tried all types of diets, including bouillon made with a **duck press.** (She never gave up pastries and ice cream, however.) After she turned 30, Sisi refused to appear in any portraits or photographs, preferring that only her more youthful depictions be preserved. Appreciate the **white gloves,** the **ivory fan,** and the **white nightgown** (displayed nearby)...because her life was about to turn even darker.

▶ *Then enter the darkest room.*

Death of Sisi's Son

A mannequin wears a replica of Sisi's **black dress,** and nearby you'll see **black jewels** and accessories. In 1889, Sisi and Franz Josef's son, Prince Rudolf—whose life had veered into sex, drugs, and liberal politics—apparently killed his lover and himself in a suicide pact. Sisi was shattered and retreated further from public life.

▶ *Stroll through several more rooms.*

Escape

Sisi consoled herself with **poetry** (the museum has quotes on the walls) that expresses a longing to escape into an ideal world. As you continue through the exhibit, you'll see she also consoled herself with travel. There's a reconstruction of her **rail car**—a step above a *couchette*. A **map** shows her visits to Britain, Eastern Europe, and her favorite spot, Greece.

Final Room: Assassination

Sisi met her fate while traveling. While walking along a street in Geneva, Sisi was stalked and attacked by an Italian anarchist who despised royal oppressors and wanted notoriety for his cause. (He'd planned on assassinating a less-famous French prince that day—whom he'd been unable to track down—but quickly changed plans when word got out that Sisi was in town.) The **murder weapon** was this small, crude, knife-like file. It made only a small wound, but it proved fatal.

▶ *After the Sisi Museum, a one-way route takes you through a series of royal rooms. The first room—as if to make clear that there was more to the Habsburgs than Sisi—shows a family tree tracing the Habsburgs from 1273 (Rudolf I at upper left) to their messy WWI demise (Karl I, lower right). From here, enter the private apartments of the royal family (Franz Josef's first, then Sisi's). Much of the following commentary complements the information you'll hear in the audioguide.*

Imperial Apartments

These were the private apartments and public meeting rooms for the emperor and empress. Franz Josef I lived here from 1857 until his death in 1916. (He had hoped to move to new digs in the New Palace, but that was not finished until after his death.)

Franz Josef was the last great Habsburg ruler. In these rooms, he presided over defeats and liberal inroads as the world was changing and the monarchy becoming obsolete. Here he met with advisors and welcomed foreign dignitaries; hosted lavish, white-gloved balls and stuffy formal dinners; and raised three children. He slept (alone) on his austere bed while his beloved wife Sisi retreated to her own rooms. He suffered through the

Each of the rooms features a different variation on chandeliered, stuccoed opulence.

execution of his brother, the suicide of his son and heir, the murder of his wife, and the assassination of his nephew, Archduke Ferdinand, which sparked World War I and spelled the end of the Habsburg monarchy

The Emperor's Rooms

Waiting Room for the Audience Room

Every citizen had the right to meet privately with the emperor, and people traveled fairly far to do so. While they waited nervously, they had these **three huge paintings** to stare at—propaganda showing crowds of commoners enthusiastic about their Habsburg rulers.

The painting on the right shows an 1809 scene of Emperor Franz II (Franz Josef's grandfather) returning to Vienna, celebrating the news that Napoleon had begun his retreat.

In the central painting, Franz II makes his first public appearance to adoring crowds after recovering from a life-threatening illness (1826).

In the painting on the left, Franz II returns to Vienna (see the Karlskirche in the background) to celebrate the defeat of Napoleon. The 1815 Congress of Vienna that followed was the greatest assembly of

Emperor Franz Josef (1830-1916)

Franz Josef I—who ruled for 68 years (1848-1916)—was the embodiment of the Habsburg Empire as it finished its six-century-long ride. Born in 1830, Franz Josef had a stern upbringing that instilled in him a powerful sense of duty and—like so many men of power—a love of all things military.

As the revolutions of 1848 rattled royal families throughout Europe, the Habsburgs forced feeble Ferdinand to abdicate and put 18-year-old Franz Josef on the throne. Ironically, one of his first acts was to crush Hungarian freedom fighters with bloody harshness. Rather than acknowledge the changing world around him, Franz Josef became very conservative. But worse, he wrongly believed he was a talented military tactician, leading Austria into catastrophic battles against Italy.

Wearing his uniform to the end, Franz Josef never saw what a dinosaur his monarchy was becoming. He had no interest in democracy and pointedly never set foot in Austria's parliament building. Like his contemporary Queen Victoria, he was a microcosm of his empire—old-fashioned but sacrosanct. Mired in his passion for low-grade paperwork (which earned him the nickname "Joe Bureaucrat"), he missed the big picture. In 1914, he helped start a Great War that ultimately ended the age of monarchs.

diplomats in European history. Its goal: to establish peace by shoring up Europe's monarchies against the rise of democracy and nationalism. It worked for about a century, until a colossal war—World War I—wiped out the Habsburgs and other European royal families.

This room's **chandelier**—considered the best in the palace—is Baroque, made of Bohemian crystal. It lit things until 1891, when the palace installed electric lights.

Audience Chamber

This is the room where Franz Josef received commoners from around the empire. Imagine you've traveled for days to have your say before the emperor. You're wearing your new fancy suit—Franz Josef required that men coming before him wear a tailcoat, women a black gown with a train. You've rehearsed what you want to say. You hope your hair looks good.

Suddenly, you're face-to-face with the emp himself. (The **portrait** on the easel shows Franz Josef in 1915, when he was more than 80 years old.) He'd stand at the **lectern** (far left) as the visiting commoners had their say (but for no more than two and a half minutes). Standing kept things moving. You'd hear a brief response from him (quite likely the same he'd given all day), and then you'd back out of the room while bowing (also required). On the lectern is a partial **list** of 56 appointments he had on January 3, 1910 (three columns: family name, meeting topic, and *Anmerkung*—the emperor's "action log").

Conference Room

The emperor and his cabinet sat at this long Empire-style table to discuss policy. An ongoing topic was what to do with unruly Hungary. After 1867, Franz Josef granted Hungary a measure of independence (thus creating the "Austro-Hungarian Empire"). Hungarian diplomats attended meetings here, watched over by **paintings** on the wall showing Austria's army suppressing the popular Hungarian uprising… subtle.

Emperor Franz Josef's Study

This room evokes how seriously the emperor took his responsibilities as the top official of a vast empire. Famously energetic, Franz Josef lived a spartan life dedicated to duty. The **desk** was originally positioned in such a way that Franz Josef could look up from his work and see the **portrait** of his lovely, long-haired, tiny-waisted Empress Elisabeth reflected in the mirror. Notice the **trompe l'oeil paintings** above each door, giving the believable illusion of marble relief. Notice also all the **family photos**—the perfect gift for the dad/uncle/hubby who has it all.

The walls between the rooms are wide enough to hide servants' corridors (the hidden door to his valet's room is in the back-left corner). The emperor lived with a personal staff of 14: "three valets, four lackeys, two doormen, two manservants, and three chambermaids."

Franz Josef adored Sisi, and kept reminders of her everywhere—like on his office desk.

Emperor's Bedroom

Franz Josef famously slept on this no-frills **iron bed** and used the **portable washstand** until 1880 (when the palace got running water). He typically rose before dawn and started his day in prayer, kneeling at the **prayer stool** against the far wall. After all, he was a "Divine Right" ruler. While he had a typical emperor's share of mistresses, his dresser was always well-stocked with **photos** of Sisi. Franz Josef lived here after his estrangement from Sisi. An **etching** shows the empress—a fine rider and avid hunter—sitting sidesaddle while jumping a hedge.

Large Salon

This red-walled room was for royal family gatherings and went unused after Sisi's death. The big, ornate **stove** in the corner was fed from behind (this remained a standard form of heating through the 19th century).

Small Salon

This room is dedicated to the memory of Franz Josef's brother (see the **portrait with the weird beard**), the Emperor Maximilian I of Mexico, who was overthrown and executed in 1867. It was also a smoking room. This was a necessity in the early 19th century, when smoking was newly fashionable for men, and was never done in the presence of women.

After the birth of their last child in 1868, Franz Josef and Sisi began to drift further apart. Left of the door is a small **button** the emperor had to buzz before entering his estranged wife's quarters. You, however, can go right in.

▶ *Climb three steps and enter Sisi's wing.*

Empress' Rooms

Empress' Bedroom and Drawing Room

This was Sisi's room, refurbished in the Neo-Rococo style in 1854. There's the red **carpet,** covered with oriental rugs. The room always had lots of fresh flowers. Sisi not only slept here, but also lived here—the bed was rolled in and out daily—until her death in 1898. The **desk** is where she sat and wrote her letters and sad poems.

Empress' Dressing/Exercise Room

Servants worked three hours a day on Sisi's famous hair, while she passed the time reading and learning Hungarian. She'd exercise on the **wooden**

Carpets, divans, and ceramic furnaces (like those on the right) gave state-of-the-art comfort.

structure and on the **rings** suspended from the doorway to the left. Afterward, she'd get a massage on the red-covered **bed.** You can psychoanalyze Sisi from the **portraits and photos** she chose to hang on her walls. They're mostly her favorite dogs, her Bavarian family, and several portraits of the romantic and anti-monarchist poet Heinrich Heine. Her infatuation with the liberal Heine, whose family was Jewish, caused a stir in royal circles.

Empress' Lavatory and Bathroom

Detour into the behind-the-scenes palace. In the narrow passageway, you'll walk by Sisi's hand-painted porcelain, dolphin-head **WC** (on the right). The big tank left of the tub warmed her towels. In the main bathroom, you'll see her huge copper tub (with the original wall coverings behind it), where servants washed her hair. Sisi was the first Habsburg to have running water in her bathroom (notice the hot and cold faucets). Beneath the carpet you're walking on is the first linoleum ever used in Vienna (c. 1880).

Servants' Quarters (Bergl Rooms)

Next, enter the servants' quarters, with hand-painted **tropical scenes.**

Take time to enjoy the playful details. As you leave these rooms and re-enter the imperial world, look back to the room on the left.

Empress' Large Salon

The room is **painted** with Mediterranean escapes, the 19th-century equivalent of travel posters. The **statue of Polyhymnia** (the mythical Muse of poetry) is by the great Neoclassical master Antonio Canova. It has the features of Elisa, Napoleon's oldest sister, who hobnobbed with the Habsburgs. A **print** shows how Franz Josef and Sisi would—on their good days—share breakfast in this room.

Small Salon

The portrait is of **Crown Prince Rudolf,** Franz Josef's and Sisi's only son. On the morning of January 30, 1889, the 30-year-old Rudolf and a beautiful baroness were found shot dead in his hunting lodge in Mayerling. An investigation never came up with a complete explanation, but Rudolf had obviously been cheating on his wife, and the affair ended in an apparent murder-suicide. The scandal shocked the empire and tainted the Habsburgs; Sisi retreated further into her fantasy world, and Franz Josef carried on stoically with a broken heart. The mysterious "Mayerling Affair" has been dramatized in numerous movies, plays, an opera, and even a ballet.

▶ *Leaving Sisi's wing, turn the corner into the white and gold rooms occupied by the czar of Russia during the 1814-1815 Congress of Vienna. Sisi and Franz Josef used the rooms for formal occasions and public functions.*

Alexander Apartments

Red Salon

The Gobelin wall hangings were a 1776 gift from Marie-Antoinette and Louis XVI in Paris to their Viennese counterparts.

Dining Room

It's dinnertime, and Franz Josef has called his extended family together. The settings are modest...just silver. Gold was saved for formal state dinners. Next to each name card was a menu listing the chef responsible for each dish. (Talk about pressure.) While the Hofburg had tableware

The dining room hosted both heads of state as well as the emperor's large extended family.

for 4,000, feeding 3,000 was a typical day. The cellar was stocked with 60,000 bottles of wine. The kitchen was huge—50 birds could be roasted at once on the hand-driven spits.

The emperor sat in the center of the long table. "Ladies and gentle-men" alternated in the seating. The green glasses were specifically for Rhenish wine (dry whites from the Rhine valley). Franz Josef enforced strict protocol at mealtime: No one could speak without being spoken to by the emperor, and no one could eat after he was done. While the rest of Europe was growing democracy and expanding personal freedoms, the Habsburgs preserved their ossified worldview to the bitter end.

In 1918, World War I ended, Austria was created as a modern nation-state, the Habsburgs were tossed out...and Hofburg Palace was destined to become a museum.

▶ *Drop off your audioguide, zip through the shop, go down the stairs, and you're back on the street. Two quick lefts take you back to the palace square (In der Burg), where the Treasury awaits just past the black, red, and gold gate on the far side (see the next chapter).*

Hofburg Treasury Tour

The Hofburg Palace's Imperial Treasury contains the best jewels on the Continent. Slip through the vault doors and reflect on the glitter of 21 rooms filled with secular and religious ornaments, scepters, swords, crowns, orbs, weighty robes, double-headed eagles, gowns, gem-studded bangles, and a unicorn horn.

There are plenty of beautiful objects here—I've highlighted those that have the most history behind them. But you could spend days in here marveling at the riches of the bygone empire.

Use this chapter to get the lay of the land, but rent the excellent audioguide to really delve into the Treasury.

ORIENTATION

Cost: €12, €20 combo-ticket with Kunsthistorisches Museum.

Hours: Wed-Mon 9:00-17:30, closed Tue.

Information: Tel. 01/525-240, www.kaiserliche-schatzkammer.at.

Getting There: The Treasury is tucked away in the Hofburg Palace complex. From the Hofburg's central courtyard (In der Burg), salute the Caesar-esque statue and turn about-face. Pass through the black, red, and gold gate (Schweizertor), following *Schatzkammer* signs, which lead into the Schweizerhof courtyard; the Treasury entrance is in the far-right corner. Follow signs to a stairway that climbs up to the Treasury. (See map on page 68.)

Tours: The €4 audioguide (€7/2 people) describes 100 stops—well worth it to get the most out of this dazzling collection. Guided tours (€3) leave at 14:00 every day the Treasury's open.

Starring: The Imperial Crown and other accessories of the Holy Roman Emperors, plus many other crowns, jewels, robes, and priceless knickknacks.

THE TOUR BEGINS

The Habsburgs saw themselves as the successors to the ancient Roman emperors, and they wanted crowns and royal regalia to match the pomp of the ancients. They used these precious objects for coronation ceremonies, official ribbon-cutting events, and their own personal pleasure. You'll see the prestigious crowns and accoutrements of the rulers of the Holy Roman Empire (a medieval alliance of Germanic kingdoms so named because it wanted to be considered the continuation of the Roman Empire). Other crowns belonged to Austrian dukes and kings, and some robes and paraphernalia were used by Austria's religious elite. And many costly things were created simply for the enjoyment of the wealthy (but not necessarily royal) Habsburgs.

▶ *Skip through Room 1 to where we'll begin, in Room 2.*

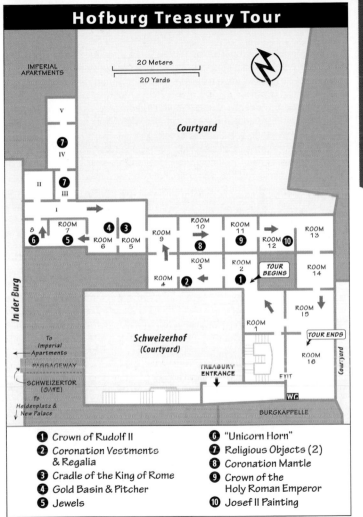

Hofburg Treasury Tour

IMPERIAL
APARTMENTS

20 Meters

20 Yards

Courtyard

V

7

IV

II

7

III

I

ROOM
7

8

6

5

ROOM
6

ROOM
5

4 **3**

ROOM
9

ROOM
10

8

ROOM
3

ROOM
4

2

ROOM
11

9

ROOM
2

1

TOUR
BEGINS

ROOM
12

10

ROOM
13

ROOM
14

Schweizerhof
(Courtyard)

In der Burg

To
Imperial
Apartments

BAGGAGEWAY

SCHWEIZERTOR
(GATE)

To
Heidenplatz &
New Palace

TREASURY
ENTRANCE

ROOM
1

EXIT

WC

BURGKAPELLE

ROOM
15

TOUR ENDS

ROOM
16

Camp Camp

1 Crown of Rudolf II

2 Coronation Vestments
& Regalia

3 Cradle of the King of Rome

4 Gold Basin & Pitcher

5 Jewels

6 "Unicorn Horn"

7 Religious Objects (2)

8 Coronation Mantle

9 Crown of the
Holy Roman Emperor

10 Josef II Painting

From the First Habsburg to Napoleon

Room 2

The personal ❶ **crown of Rudolf II** (1602) occupies the center of the room along with its accompanying scepter and orb; a bust of Rudolf II (1552-1612) sits nearby. The crown's design symbolically merges a bishop's miter ("Holy"), the arch across the top of a Roman emperor's helmet ("Roman"), and the typical medieval king's crown ("Emperor"). Accompanying the crown are the matching **scepter** (made from the ivory tusk of a narwhal) and **orb** (holding four diamonds to symbolize the four corners of the world, which the emperor ruled). Orbs have been royal symbols of the world since ancient Roman times. They seem to indicate that, even in pre-Columbus days, Europe's intelligentsia assumed the world was round.

This crown was Rudolf's personal one. He wore a different crown (which we'll see later) in his official role as Holy Roman Emperor. In many dynasties, a personal crown like this was dismantled by the next ruler to custom-make his own. But Rudolf's crown was so well-crafted that it was passed down through the generations, even inspiring crown-shaped church steeples as far away as Amsterdam (when that city was under Habsburg control).

Two centuries later (1806), this crown and scepter became the official regalia of Austria's rulers, as seen in the large **portrait of Franz I** (the open-legged guy behind you). Napoleon Bonaparte had just conquered Austria and dissolved the Holy Roman Empire. Franz (r. 1792-1835) was allowed to remain in power, but he had to downgrade his title from "Franz II, Holy Roman Emperor" to "Franz I, Emperor of Austria."

The crown of Rudolf II

Napoleon's son's luxurious cradle

Rooms 3 and 4

These rooms contain some of the ❷ **coronation vestments and regalia** needed for the new Austrian (not Holy Roman) Emperor. There was a different one for each of the emperor's subsidiary titles, e.g., King of Hungary or King of Lombardy. So many crowns and kingdoms in the Habsburgs' vast empire! Those with the white ermine collars are modeled after Napoleon's coronation robes.

▶ For more on how Napoleon had an impact on Habsburg Austria, pass through Room 9 and into...

Room 5

Ponder the ❸ **Cradle of the King of Rome,** once occupied by Napoleon's son, who was born in 1811 and made King of Rome. The little eagle at the foot is symbolically not yet able to fly, but glory-bound. Glory is symbolized by the star, with dad's big *N* raised high. While it's fun to think of Napoleon's baby snoozing in here, this was a ceremonial "throne bed" that was rarely used.

Napoleon Bonaparte (1769-1821) was a French commoner who rose to power as a charismatic general in the Revolution. While pledging allegiance to democracy, he in fact crowned himself Emperor of France and hobnobbed with Europe's royalty. When his wife Josephine could not bear him a male heir, Napoleon divorced her and married into the Habsburg family.

Portraits show Napoleon and his new bride, Marie Louise, Franz I/II's daughter (and Marie-Antoinette's great-niece). Napoleon gave her a **jewel chest** decorated with the bees of industriousness, his personal emblem. With the birth of the baby King of Rome, Napoleon and Marie Louise were poised to start a new dynasty of European rulers...but then Napoleon met his Waterloo, and the Habsburgs remained in power.

Miscellaneous Wonders

Room 6

For Divine Right kings, even child-rearing was a sacred ritual that needed elaborate regalia for public ceremonies. The 23-pound ❹ **gold basin and pitcher** were used to baptize noble children, who were dressed in the **baptismal dresses** displayed nearby.

Room 7

These ⑤ **jewels** are the true "treasures," a cabinet of wonders used by Habsburgs to impress their relatives (or to hock when funds got low). The irregularly shaped, 2,680-karat **emerald** is rough-cut, as the cutter wanted to do only the minimum to avoid making a mistake and shattering the giant gem. Check out the **"milk opal,"** the **"hair amethyst,"** and a 492-karat **aquamarine.** The helmet-like, jewel-studded **crown** (left wall) was a gift from Muslim Turks supporting a Hungarian king who, as a Protestant, was a thorn in the side of the Catholic Habsburgs (who eventually toppled him).

Room 8

The eight-foot-tall, 500-year-old ⑥ **"unicorn horn"** (actually a narwhal tusk), was considered to have magical healing powers bestowed from on high. This one was owned by the Holy Roman Emperor—clearly a divine monarch. The huge **agate bowl,** cut from a single piece, may have been made in ancient Roman times and eventually found its way into the collection of their successors, the Habsburgs.

Religious Rooms

After Room 8, you enter several rooms of ⑦ **religious objects**—crucifixes, chalices, mini-altarpieces, reliquaries, and bishops' vestments. Like the medieval kings who preceded them, Habsburg rulers mixed the institutions of church and state, so these precious religious accoutrements were also part of their display of secular power.

▶ *Browse these rooms, then backtrack, passing by the Cradle of the King of Rome, and eventually reaching...*

 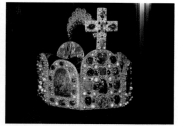

New kings were draped in this mantle...   ...and crowned with a 10th-century crown.

Regalia of the Holy Roman Empire

Room 10

The next few rooms contain some of the oldest and most venerated objects in the Treasury—the robes, crowns, and sacred objects of the Holy Roman Emperor.

The ❽ big red-silk and gold-thread **mantle,** nearly 900 years old, was worn by Holy Roman Emperors at their coronations. Notice the oriental imagery: a palm tree in the center, flanked by lions subduing camels. The hem is written in Arabic (wishing its wearer "great wealth, gifts, and pleasure"). This robe, brought back from the East by Crusaders, gave the Germanic emperors an exotic look that recalled great biblical kings such as Solomon. Many Holy Roman Emperors were crowned by the pope himself. That fact, plus this Eastern-looking mantle, helped put the "Holy" in Holy Roman Emperor.

Room 11

The collection's highlight is the ❾ 10th-century **crown of the Holy Roman Emperor.** It was probably made for Otto I (c. 960), the first king to call himself Holy Roman Emperor.

The Imperial Crown swirls with symbolism "proving" that the emperor was both holy and Roman: The cross on top says the HRE ruled as Christ's representative on earth, and the jeweled arch over the top is reminiscent of the parade helmet of ancient Romans. The jewels themselves allude to the wearer's kinghood in the here and now. Imagine the impression this priceless, glittering crown must have made on the emperor's medieval subjects.

King Solomon's portrait on the crown (to the right of the cross) is Old Testament proof that kings can be wise and good. King David (next panel) is similar proof that they can be just. The crown's eight sides represent the celestial city of Jerusalem's eight gates. The jewels on the front panel symbolize the 12 apostles.

On the forehead of the crown, notice that beneath the cross there's a pale-blue, heart-shaped sapphire. Look a little small for the prime spot? That's because this is a replacement for a long-lost opal said to have had almost mythical, magical powers.

Nearby is the 11th-century **Imperial Cross** that preceded the emperor in ceremonies. Encrusted with jewels, it had a hollow compartment (its core is wood) that carried substantial chunks thought to be from *the*

Charlemagne and the Holy Roman Empire

The title "Holy Roman Emperor" conveyed three important concepts: **Holy,** meaning the emperor ruled by divine authority (and not as a pagan Roman); **Roman,** indicating he was a successor to the ancient Roman Empire; and **Emperor,** meaning he ruled over many different nationalities.

Charlemagne (747-814) briefly united much of Western Europe—that is, the former Roman Empire. On Christmas Eve in the year 800, he was crowned "Roman Emperor" by the pope in St. Peter's Basilica in Rome. After Charlemagne's death, the empire split apart. His successors (who ruled only a portion of Charlemagne's empire) still wanted to envision themselves as inheritors of Charlemagne's greatness. They took to calling themselves Roman Emperors, adding the "Holy" part in the 11th century to emphasize that they ruled by divine authority.

The Holy Roman Emperorship was an elected, not necessarily hereditary, office. Traditionally, four dukes and three archbishops (called Electors) convened to pick the new ruler—who was usually a Habsburg. At the empire's peak around 1520, Emperor Charles V ruled lands stretching from Vienna to Spain, from Holland to Sicily, and from Bohemia to Bolivia in the New World. But throughout much of its existence, the HRE consisted of little more than petty dukes ruling a loose coalition of independent nobles. It was Voltaire who quipped that the HRE was "neither holy, nor Roman, nor an empire."

Napoleon ended the title in 1806. The last Habsburg emperors (including Franz Josef) were merely emperors of Austria.

cross on which Jesus was crucified and *the* Holy Lance used to pierce his side (both pieces are displayed in the same glass case). Holy Roman Emperors actually carried the lance into battle in the 10th century. Look behind the cross to see how it was a box that could be clipped open and shut, used for holding holy relics. You can see bits of the "true cross" anywhere, but this is a prime piece—with the actual nail hole.

Another case has additional objects used in the coronation ceremony: The **orb** (orbs were modeled on late-Roman ceremonial objects, then topped with the cross) and **scepter** (the one with the oak leaves), along with the sword, were carried ahead of the emperor in the procession. In earlier times, these objects were thought to have belonged to Charlemagne himself, the greatest ruler of medieval Europe, but in fact they're mostly from 300 to 400 years later (c. 1200).

Yet another glass case contains more objects said to belong to Charlemagne. Some of these may be authentic, since they're closer to his era. You'll see the jeweled, purse-like **reliquary of St. Stephen** and the **saber of Charlemagne.** The gold-covered **Book of the Gospels** was the Bible that emperors placed their hands on to swear the oath of office. On the wall nearby, the **tall painting** depicts Charlemagne modeling the Imperial Crown—although the crown wasn't made until a hundred years after he died.

Room 12

Now picture all this regalia used together. The ❿ **painting** shows the coronation of Maria Theresa's son Josef II as Holy Roman Emperor in 1764. Set in a church in Frankfurt (filled with the bigwigs—literally—of the day), Josef is wearing the same crown and royal garb that you've just seen.

Emperors followed the same coronation ritual that originated in the 10th century. The new emperor would don the mantle. The entourage paraded into a church for Mass, led by the religious authorities carrying the Imperial Cross. The emperor placed his hand on the Book of the Gospels and swore his oath. Then he knelt before the three archbishop Electors, who placed the Imperial Crown on his head (sometimes he even traveled to Rome to be crowned by the pope himself). The new emperor rose, accepted the orb and scepter, and—dut dutta dah!—you had a new ruler.

▶ *The tour is over. Pass through Rooms 13-16 to reach the exit, browsing relics, portraits, and objects along the way.*

Kunsthistorisches Museum Tour

The Kunsthistorwhatoveritis Museum—let's just say "Kunst" (koonst)—houses the family collection of Austria's luxury-loving Habsburg rulers. Their joie de vivre is reflected in this collection—some of the most beautiful, sexy, and fun art from two centuries (c. 1450-1650). At their peak of power in the 1500s, the Habsburgs ruled Austria, Germany, northern Italy, the Netherlands, and Spain—and you'll see a wide variety of art from all these places and beyond.

The building itself is worth notice—a lavish textbook example of Historicism. Despite its palatial feel, it was originally designed for the same purpose it serves today: to showcase its treasures in an inviting space while impressing visitors with the grandeur of the empire.

A statue of Maria Theresa watches over the Kunsthistorisches Museum and its eclectic art collection.

ORIENTATION

Cost: €15, free for kids under age 19, €20 combo-ticket includes the Hofburg Treasury.

Hours: Daily 10:00-18:00, Thu until 21:00, closed Mon in Sept-May.

Information: Tel. 01/525-240, www.khm.at.

Getting There: It's on the Ringstrasse at Maria-Theresien-Platz, U: Volkstheater/Museumsplatz (exit toward *Burgring*).

Tours: The excellent €4 audioguide, covering nearly 600 items, is worthwhile if you want an in-depth tour beyond the items covered in this chapter.

Services: There's a free cloakroom. The restaurant is on the first floor.

Starring: The world's best collection of Bruegel, plus Titian, Caravaggio, a Vermeer gem, and Rembrandt self-portraits.

THE TOUR BEGINS

Of the museum's many exhibits, we'll tour only the Painting Gallery (Gemäldegalerie) on the first floor. Italian-Spanish-French art is on one half of the floor, and Northern European art on the other. On our tour, we'll get a sampling of each. Note that the museum labels the largest rooms with Roman numerals (Saal I, II, III) and the smaller rooms around the perimeter with Arabic (Rooms 1, 2, 3). The museum seems to constantly move paintings from room to room, so be flexible.

▶ *Climb the main staircase, featuring Antonio Canova's statue of Theseus clubbing a centaur. Bear right when you reach Theseus. At the top of the staircase, make a U-turn to the left. Enter Saal I and walk right into the High Renaissance.*

Italian Renaissance

About the year 1500, Italy was in the midst of a 100-year renaissance, or "rebirth," of interest in the art and learning of ancient Greece and Rome. In painting, that meant that ordinary humans and Greek gods joined saints and angels as popular subjects.

Titian, *Danae* and *Ecce Homo*

In the long career of Titian the Venetian (it rhymes), he painted portraits, Christian Madonnas, and sexy Venuses with equal ease.

Titian captured Danae—a luscious nude reclining in bed—as she's about to be seduced. Zeus, the king of the gods, descends as a shower of gold to consort with her—you can almost see the human form of Zeus within the cloud. Danae is helpless with rapture, opening her legs to receive

Canova's statue guides you to the paintings.

Titian's *Danaë*—a Renaissance centerfold

Kunsthistorisches Museum—First Floor

ROOM 17 REMBRANDT

ROOM 16

ROOM 15

ROOM 14

SAA

TEMPORARY

WC

VERMEER ROOM 18

SAAL XI

SAAL X

BRUEGEL

TOUR ENDS

SAAL IX

STAIRS TO SECOND FLOOR

THESEU STATUE

ROOM 19

SAAL XII

NORTHERN EUROPEAN ART

STAIRS FROM GROUND FLOO

ROOM 20

SAAL XIII

SAAL XIV

RUBENS

SAAL XV DÜRER

ROOM 21

ROOM 22

ROOM 23

ROOM 24

To Ringstrasse

MAI

Maria-Theresien-

him, while her servant tries to catch the heavenly spurt with a golden dish. Danae's rich, luminous flesh is set off by the dark servant at right and the threatening sky above. The white sheets beneath her make her glow even more. This is not just a classic nude—it's a Renaissance Miss August. How could ultra-conservative Catholic emperors have tolerated such a downright pagan and erotic painting? Apparently, without a problem.

In the large canvas *Ecce Homo,* a crowd mills about, when suddenly

there's a commotion. They nudge each other and start to point. Follow their gaze diagonally up the stairs to a battered figure entering way up in the corner. "Ecce Homo!" says Pilate. "Behold the man." And he presents Jesus to the mob. For us, as for the unsympathetic crowd, the humiliated Son of God is not the center of the scene, but almost an afterthought.

▶ Continue to Saal III.

Raphael, *Madonna of the Meadow*

Young Raphael epitomized the spirit of the High Renaissance, combining symmetry, grace, beauty, and emotion. This Madonna is a mountain of motherly love—Mary's head is the summit and her flowing robe is the base—enfolding Baby Jesus and John the Baptist. The geometric perfection, serene landscape, and Mary's adoring face make this a masterpiece of sheer grace—but then you get smacked by an ironic fist: The cross the little tykes play with foreshadows their gruesome deaths.

▶ *Before moving on, be aware that the Kunst displays excellent small canvases in the smaller side rooms. For example, in Rooms 1-3, you*

The Habsburgs loved beauty—like Raphael's creamy *Madonna* in a harmonic pyramid pose.

Parmigianino poses for himself—say cheese!

One of Arcimboldo's fruity faces

may find **Correggio's Jupiter and Io,** *showing Zeus seducing another female, this time disguised as a cloud.* **Parmigianino's Self-Portrait in a Convex Mirror** *depicts the artist gazing into a convex mirror and perfectly reproducing the curved reflection on a convex piece of wood. Amazing.*

Farther along, through the small rooms along the far end of this wing (and likely in Room 6), find...

Arcimboldo, Portraits of the Seasons

These four cleverly deceptive portraits by the Habsburg court painter depict the four seasons (and elements) as people. For example, take *Summer*—a.k.a. "Fruit Face." With a pickle nose, pear chin, and corn-husk ears, this guy literally is what he eats. Its grotesque weirdness makes it typical of Mannerist art.

▶ *Find Caravaggio in Saal V.*

Caravaggio, *Madonna of the Rosary* and *David with the Head of Goliath*

Caravaggio shocked the art world with brutally honest reality. Compared with Raphael's super-sweet *Madonna of the Meadow*, Caravaggio's *Madonna of the Rosary* (the biggest canvas in the room) looks perfectly ordinary, and the saints kneeling around her have dirty feet.

In *David with the Head of Goliath*, Caravaggio turns a third-degree-interrogation light on a familiar Bible story. David shoves the dripping head of the slain giant right in our noses. The painting, bled of color, is virtually a black-and-white crime-scene photo—slightly overexposed. Out of the

Caravaggio paints an unheroic David, stark shadows, and the artist himself in a severed head.

deep darkness shine only a few crucial details. This David is not a heroic Renaissance man like Michelangelo's famous statue, but a homeless teen that Caravaggio paid to portray God's servant. And the severed head of Goliath is none other than Caravaggio himself, an in-your-face self-portrait.

▶ *Move into Room 10, in the corner of the museum.*

Velázquez, Habsburg Family Portraits

When the Habsburgs ruled both Austria and Spain, cousins kept in touch through portraits of themselves and their kids. Diego Velázquez was the greatest of Spain's "photojournalist" painters—heavily influenced by Caravaggio's realism, capturing his subjects without passing judgment, flattering, or glorifying them.

For example, watch little Margarita Habsburg grow up in three different portraits, from age two to age nine. Margarita was destined from birth to marry her Austrian cousin, the future Emperor Leopold I. Pictures like these, sent from Spain every few years, let her pen pal/fiancé get to know her.

Also see a portrait of Margarita's little brother, *Philip Prosper,* wearing a dress. Sadly, Philip was a sickly boy who would only live two years longer. The amulets he's wearing were intended to fend off illness. His hand rests limply on the back of the chair—above an adorable puppy who seems to be asking, "But who will play with me?"

The kids' oh-so-serious faces, regal poses, and royal trappings are contradicted by their natural precociousness. No wonder Velázquez was so popular.

Also notice that all of these kids are quite, ahem, homely. To understand why, find the portrait of their dad, Philip IV, which shows the defects

It's easy to see the Habsburg family resemblance in Velázquez's many royal portraits.

of royal inbreeding: weepy eyes and a pointed chin (sorry, that pointy moustache doesn't hide anything).

▶ *Return to the main Saals and continue on, past glimpses of Baroque art, featuring large, colorful canvases showcasing over-the-top emotions and pudgy, winged babies (the surefire mark of Baroque art). In Saal VII, find paintings of the Habsburg summer palace, Schloss Schönbrunn, by* **Canaletto,** *one of which also shows the Viennese skyline in the distance.*

Exit Saal VII. Cross the stairwell and enter Saal XV, in the part of the museum dedicated to Northern art.

Northern Art

The "Northern Renaissance," brought on by the economic boom of Dutch and Flemish trading, was more secular and Protestant than Catholic-funded Italian art. We'll see fewer Madonnas, saints, and Greek gods and more peasants, landscapes, and food. Paintings are smaller and darker, full of down-to-earth objects. Northern artists sweated the details, encouraging the patient viewer to appreciate the beauty in everyday things.

Dürer had Italian Renaissance training. He composes many figures into geometrical harmony.

Hélène Fourment, teenage wife...

...of middle-aged Rubens

Dürer, Landauer Altarpiece

As the son of a goldsmith and having traveled to Italy, Albrecht Dürer combined meticulous Northern detail with Renaissance symmetry. So this altarpiece may initially look like a complex hog pile of saints and angels, but it's perfectly geometrical. The crucified Christ forms a triangle in the center, framed by triangular clouds and flanked by three-sided crowds of people—appropriate for a painting about the Trinity. Dürer practically invented the self-portrait as an art form, and he included himself, the lone earthling in this heavenly vision (bottom right), with a plaque announcing that he, Albrecht Dürer, painted this in 1511.

▶ *Now enter the big-canvas, bright-colored world of Baroque in Saals XIV and XIII.*

Peter Paul Rubens

Rubens' work runs the gamut, from realistic portraits to lounging nudes, Greek myths to altarpieces, from pious devotion to violent sex.

But, can we be sure it's Baroque? Ah yes, I'm sure you'll find a pudgy, winged baby somewhere, hovering in the heavens. Take the large *Ildefonso Altarpiece* (likely in Saal XIII), where a glorious Mary appears—with her entourage of PWBs—to reward the grateful Spanish St. Ildefonso with a chasuble (priest's smock).

In Rubens' *Self-Portrait,* admire the darling of Catholic-dominated Flanders (northern Belgium) in his prime: famous, wealthy, well-traveled, the friend of kings and princes, an artist, diplomat, man about town, and—obviously—confident.

The 53-year-old Rubens married Hélène Fourment, a dimpled girl of 16 (find her portrait nearby). She pulls the fur around her ample flesh,

Rubens' huge canvases, such as *The Miracles of St. Francis Xavier,* dwarf visitors.

simultaneously covering herself and exalting her charms. Rubens called this painting *The Little Fur*—and used the same name for his young bride. Hmm. Hélène's sweet cellulite was surely an inspiration to Rubens—many of his female figures have Hélène's gentle face and dimpled proportions.

How could Rubens paint all these enormous canvases in one lifetime? He didn't. He kept a workshop of assistants busy painting backgrounds and minor figures, working from his own small sketches. Then the master stepped in to add the finishing touches. For example, the giant canvas *The Miracles of St. Ignatius of Loyola* was painted partly by assistants, guided by Rubens' sketches (likely displayed nearby).

▶ *Pass through several rooms until you reach Room 18, with a small jewel of a canvas by Vermeer.*

Jan Vermeer

In his small canvases, the Dutch painter Jan Vermeer quiets the world down to where we can hear our own heartbeat, letting us appreciate the beauty in common things.

Vermeer's *Art of Painting*—the curtain opens, and we see the diligent genius at work.

The curtain opens and we see *The Art of Painting*, a behind-the-scenes look at Vermeer at work. He's painting a model dressed in blue, starting with her laurel-leaf headdress. The studio is its own little dollhouse world framed by a chair in the foreground and the wall in back. Then Vermeer fills this space with the few gems he wants us to focus on—the chandelier, the map, the painter's costume. Everything is lit by a crystal-clear light, letting us see these everyday items with fresh eyes.

This piece is also called *The Allegory of Painting*. The model has the laurel leaves, trumpet, and book that symbolize the muse of history and fame. The artist—his back to the public—earnestly tries to capture fleeting fame with a small sheet of canvas.

▶ *In the corner room (Room 17), find dark, brooding works by...*

Rembrandt van Rijn

Rembrandt became wealthy by painting portraits of Holland's upwardly mobile businessmen, but his greatest subject was himself. In the *Large Self-Portrait* we see the hands-on-hips, defiant, open-stance

Rembrandt—the master of self-portraits...   ...each one showing a subtle new emotion

determination of a man who will do what he wants, and if people don't like it, tough.

In typical Rembrandt style, most of the canvas is a dark, smudgy brown, with only the side of his face glowing from the darkness. (Remember Caravaggio? Rembrandt did.) Unfortunately, the year this was painted, Rembrandt's fortunes changed.

Looking at the *Small Self-Portrait* from 1657, consider Rembrandt's last years. His wife died, his children died young, and commissions for paintings dried up as his style veered from the common path. He had to auction off paintings to pay his debts, and he died a poor man. Rembrandt's numerous self-portraits painted from youth until old age show a man always changing—from wide-eyed youth to successful portraitist to this disillusioned, but still defiant, old man.

▶ *Nearby, Saal X contains the largest collection of Bruegels in captivity. Linger. If you like it, linger longer.*

Pieter Bruegel the Elder

The undisputed master of the slice-of-life village scene was Pieter Bruegel the Elder (c. 1525-1569)—think of him as the Norman Rockwell of the 16th century. His name (pronounced "BROY-gull") is sometimes spelled *Brueghel.* Don't confuse Pieter Bruegel the Elder with his sons, Pieter Brueghel the Younger and Jan Brueghel, who added luster and an "h" to the family name (and whose works are also displayed in the Kunst). Despite his many rural paintings, Bruegel was actually a cultivated urbanite who liked to wear peasants' clothing to observe country folk at play (a trans-fest-ite?). He celebrated their simple life, but he also skewered their weaknesses—not to single them out as hicks, but as universal examples of human folly.

The Peasant Wedding, Bruegel's most famous work, is less about the wedding than the food. It's a farmers' feeding frenzy, as the barnful of wedding guests scrambles to get their share of free eats. Two men bring in the next course, a tray of fresh porridge. The bagpiper pauses to check it out. A guy grabs bowls and passes them down the table, taking our attention with them. Everyone's going at it, including a kid in an oversized red cap who licks the bowl with his fingers. In the middle of it all, look who's been completely forgotten—the demure bride sitting in front of the blue-green cloth. According to Flemish tradition, the bride was not allowed to speak or eat at the party, and the groom was not in attendance at all. (One thing: The guy carrying the front end of the food tray—is he stepping forward with his right leg, or with his left, or with...all three?)

Speaking of two left feet, Bruegel's *Peasant Dance* shows a celebration at the consecration of a village church. Peasants happily clog to the

Bruegel's peasants dance, eat, drink, and sing in the Kunst's collection—the world's largest.

Bruegel's party extends beyond the frame.

A quiet scene of country life

tune of a lone bagpiper, who wails away while his pit crew keeps him lubed with wine. Notice the overexuberant guy in the green hat on the left, who accidentally smacks his buddy in the face. As with his other peasant paintings, Bruegel captures the warts-and-all scene accurately—it's neither romanticized nor patronizing.

Find several Bruegel landscape paintings. These are part of an original series of six "calendar" paintings, depicting the seasons of the year. We see these scenes from above, emphasizing the landscape as much as the people. *Gloomy Day* opens the cycle, as winter turns to spring... slowly. The snow has melted, flooding the distant river, the trees are still leafless, and the villagers stir, cutting wood and mending fences. We skip ahead to autumn in *The Return of the Herd*—still sunny, but winter's storms are fast approaching. Finally, in *Hunters in Snow* it's the dead of winter, and three dog-tired hunters with their tired dogs trudge along with only a single fox to show for their efforts. As they crest the hill, the grove of bare trees opens up to a breathtaking view—they're almost home, where they can join their mates playing hockey. Birds soar like the hunters' rising spirits—emerging from winter's work and looking ahead to a new year.

The Tower of Babel, modeled after Rome's Colosseum, stretches into the clouds, towering over the village. Impressive as it looks, on closer inspection the tower is crooked—destined eventually to tumble onto the village. Even so, the king (in the foreground) demands further work.

▶ *Our tour is over. Linger among the Bruegels. Then consider the...*

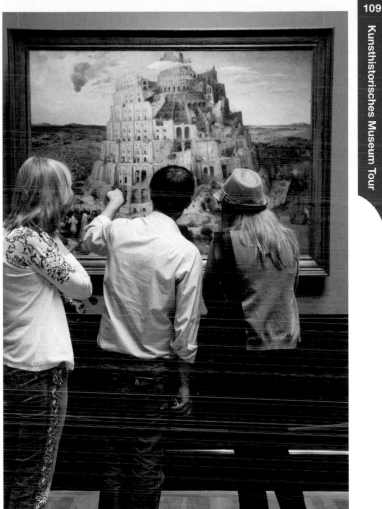

Budget time for Bruegel's colorful canvases, crammed with a thousand details worth poring over.

After seeing the paintings, kick back and enjoy luxurious objects like this tiny salt cellar.

Rest of the Kunst

We've seen only the painting half of the Kunsthistorisches Museum. The museum's ground floor has several world-class collections of Greek, Roman, Egyptian, and Near Eastern antiquities. You can see a statue of the Egyptian pharaoh Thutmosis III and the Gemma Augustea, a Roman cameo thought to be kept by Augustus on his private desk. Or view the *Kunstkammer*—the personal collections of the House of Habsburg. Amassed by 17 emperors over the centuries, the *Kunstkammer* ("art cabinet") is a dazzling display of 2,000 ancient treasures, medieval curios, and *objets d'art* from 800 to 1891. The highlight is Benvenuto Cellini's famous golden salt cellar (pictured), in Room XXIX. It was stolen in 2003 and recovered from its burial spot in the woods in 2005.

Schönbrunn Palace Tour

Among Europe's palaces, only Schönbrunn (Schloss Schönbrunn) rivals Versailles. This former summer residence of the Habsburgs is big, with more than 300 rooms in the main building alone. But don't worry—only 40 rooms are shown to the public. Of the plethora of sights at the vast complex, the highlight is a tour of the palace's Imperial Apartments—the chandeliered rooms where the Habsburg nobles lived. You can also stroll the gardens, tour the Imperial Carriage Museum, and visit a handful of lesser sights nearby.

ORIENTATION

Planning Your Time: Allow at least three hours (including transit time) for your excursion to Schönbrunn. The palace is sprawling and can be mobbed. To avoid lines, reserve your visit in advance, or use a Sisi Ticket (see "Reservations," below). After viewing the Imperial Apartments, wander the gardens (most of which are free). With more time and energy, pick and choose among the other sightseeing options and buy tickets as you go.

Cost: Visits to the palace are by timed-entry tours. The Imperial Apartments offer two tour options: The best is the 40-room **Grand Tour** ticket (€17.50, 50 minutes, includes audioguide, covered by Sisi Ticket), which includes both the rooms of Franz Josef and Sisi, as well as the (more impressive) Rococo rooms of Maria Theresa. The **Imperial Tour** (€14.20, 35 minutes, includes audioguide) covers only the less-interesting first 22 rooms. If venturing beyond the apartments, consider a combo-ticket (available mid-March-Oct only).

Hours: Imperial Apartments open daily 8:30-17:30, July-Aug until 18:30, Nov-March until 17:00; gardens generally open 6:30-20:00 but varies with season.

Information: Tel. 01/8111-3239, www.schoenbrunn.at.

Reservations: To get right in, book your entry time in advance online; tickets can also be reserved by phone at least a half-hour ahead and picked up at the visitors center. Those with a **Sisi Ticket** can enter without a reserved entry time (see page 180 for details).

Getting There: Schönbrunn is an easy 10-minute subway ride from downtown Vienna. Take U-4 (which conveniently leaves from Karlsplatz) to Schönbrunn (direction: Hütteldorf) and follow signs for *Schloss Schönbrunn.* Exit bearing right, then cross the busy road and continue to the right, to the far, far end of the long yellow building. There you'll find the visitors center, where tickets are sold.

THE TOUR BEGINS

In the 1500s, the Habsburgs built a small hunting lodge near a beautiful spring *(schön-brunn),* and for the next three centuries, they made it their summer getaway from stuffy Vienna. The palace's exterior (late 1600s) is

Baroque, but the interior was finished under Maria Theresa (mid 1700s) in let-them-eat-cake Rococo. These apartments give you a sense of the quirky, larger-than-life personalities who lived here. It's the place where matronly Maria Theresa raised her brood of 16 kids...where six-year-old Mozart played his first big gig...and where Maria Theresa's great-great-grandson Franz Josef (r. 1848-1916) tried to please his self-absorbed wife Sisi.

Your tour of the apartments, accompanied by an audioguide, follows a clearly signed one-way route. Think of the following minitour as a series of bread crumbs, leading you along while the audioguide fills in the details. Note that no photos are allowed in the Imperial Apartments.

▸ *With your ticket in hand, approach the palace. Follow signs to the entrance gate stamped on your ticket (A, B, C, etc.). When your entry time arrives, don't be shy: Politely push your way through the milling crowds to get to the ticket taker.*

Imperial Apartments

Begin in the **guards' room,** where jauntily dressed mannequins of Franz Josef's bodyguards introduce you to his luxurious world. Continue through

The backyard of the emperors' summer palace, with the Gloriette in the distance

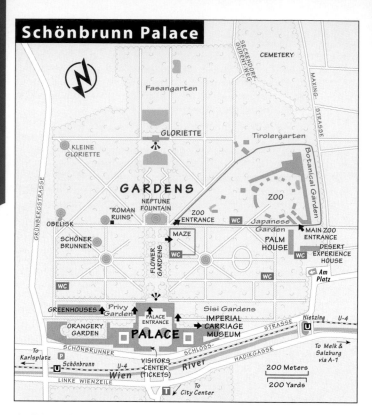

Schönbrunn Palace

CEMETERY

SECKENDORF-GUDENT-WEG

Fasangarten

MAXING STRASSE

GLORIETTE

Tirolergarten

KLEINE GLORIETTE

Botanical Garden

GARDENS

ZOO

NEPTUNE FOUNTAIN

"ROMAN RUINS"

ZOO ENTRANCE

WC

OBELISK

Japanese Garden

MAIN ZOO ENTRANCE

SCHÖNER BRUNNEN

MAZE

PALM HOUSE

DESERT EXPERIENCE HOUSE

WC

FLOWER GARDENS

WC

WC

Am Platz

GREENHOUSES

Privy Garden

Sisi Gardens

PALACE ENTRANCE

IMPERIAL CARRIAGE MUSEUM

Hietzing

U-4

ORANGERY GARDEN

PALACE

STRASSE

U

SCHÖNBRUNNER STRASSE

SCHLOSS-

HADIKGASSE

To Melk & Salzburg via A-1

To Karlsplatz

P

Schönbrunn

U-4

VISITORS CENTER (TICKETS)

River

200 Meters

200 Yards

LINKE WIENZEILE

Wien

U

To City Center

GRÜNBERGSTRASSE

the Billiard Room to the **Walnut Room.** Wow. Rococo-style wood paneling and gilding decorate this room where Franz Josef—a hard-working
modern monarch—received official visitors. Nearby is the **study**—Franz
Josef (see his mustachioed portrait) worked at this desk, sometimes joined
by his beautiful brown-haired wife Sisi (see her portrait). In the **bedcham-
ber,** where he died barely more than a century ago, a praying stool, iron
bed, and little toilet all attest to Franz Josef's spartan lifestyle (though the
paintings here remind us of the grand scale of his palace).

▶ As you turn the corner, you enter...

Empress Sisi's Study and Dressing Room

See her portrait in a black dress, as well as (a reconstruction of) the spiral staircase that once led down to her apartments. The long-haired mannequin and makeup jars in the dressing room indicate how obsessive Sisi was about her looks.

▶ *Pass through this room to reach...*

Franz Josef's and Sisi's Bedroom

The huge wood-carved double bed suggests marital bliss, but the bed is not authentic—and as for the bliss, history suggests otherwise. Nearby is **Sisi's salon.** Though this was Sisi's reception room, the pastel paintings show her husband's distinguished ancestors—the many children of Maria Theresa (including Marie-Antoinette, immediately to the left as you enter).

Follow along to the **dining room.** The whole family ate here at the huge table; today it's set with dinnerware owned by Maria Theresa and Sisi. Next is the **children's room,** with portraits of Maria Theresa (on the easel) and some of her 11 (similar-looking) daughters. The bathroom was installed for the last Habsburg empress, Zita.

▶ *Turning the corner, pass through two rooms, until you reach the...*

Many of Schönbrunn's rooms have period furniture, like the bedroom of Franz Josef and Sisi.

The lavishly stuccoed Great Gallery was the palace's main party room.

Hall of Mirrors

In this room, six-year-old Mozart performed for Maria Theresa and her family (1762). He amazed them by playing without being able to see the keys, he jumped playfully into the empress' lap, and he even asked six-year-old Marie-Antoinette to marry him.

▶ *Pass through the next room, which leads to the large, breathtaking, white-and-gold...*

Great Gallery

Imagine the parties they had here: waltzers spinning across the floor, lit by chandeliers reflecting off the mirrors, beneath stunning ceiling frescoes, while enjoying views of the gardens and the Gloriette monument (described later). When WWII bombs rained on Vienna, the palace was largely spared. It took only one direct hit—crashing through this ballroom—but, thankfully, that bomb was a dud. In 1961, President Kennedy and Soviet Premier Khrushchev met here.

▶ *Pass through the final three rooms (pausing at a painting of Maria Theresa riding a Lipizzaner horse) until you reach the...*

Hall of Ceremonies

Wedding receptions were held here, beneath a regal portrait of Maria Theresa in a pink lace dress.

▶ *If you've bought the Grand Tour ticket, you can continue on. As you prepare to leave this room, look to the left of the doorway (to the right of Maria Theresa) to find a crowded painting with (supposedly) the child Mozart (behind Plexiglass, sitting next to a priest in gray). Next you'll come to...*

More Fancy Rooms

It was in the **Blue Chinese Salon** in 1918 that the last Habsburg emperor made the decision to relinquish power. Up next, the black-lacquer **Vieux-Laque Room** may convince you the Grand Tour ticket was worth the extra euros. Continue to the **Napoleon Room.** When Napoleon conquered

It was Maria Theresa (seated at right) who made the palace interior the wonder it is today.

Austria, he took over Schönbrunn and made this his bedroom. He dumped Josephine and took a Habsburg princess as his bride, and they had a son (cutely pictured holding a wreath of flowers).

▶ *Turn the corner through the Porcelain Room and enter the stunning...*

Millions Room

Admire the rosewood paneling inset with little painted scenes, and see how the mirrors reflect to infinity.

▶ *We're nearing the end. Pass through three (admittedly gorgeous) rooms, and turn the corner into the...*

Rich Bedchamber

This darkened room has what may have been Maria Theresa's wedding bed, where she and her husband Franz produced 16 children. Then comes their **study,** with a fitting end to this palace tour—a painting showing the happy couple who left their mark all over Schönbrunn. Maria Theresa and Franz are surrounded by their brood. Imagine these kids growing up here, riding horses, frolicking in the gardens, and preparing to marry fellow royals in order to bring peace and prosperity to the happy house of Habsburg.

Palace Gardens and Nearby Sights

The large, manicured grounds fill the palace's backyard, dominated by a hill-topping monument called the Gloriette. It's a delightful, sprawling place to wander—especially on a sunny day. You can spend hours here, enjoying the views and the people-watching. And most of the park is free, as it has been for more than two centuries (open daily sunrise to dusk, entrance on either side of the palace). Note that a number of specialty features in the gardens charge admission.

Next door to the palace grounds is the world's oldest **zoo** *(Tiergarten),* built in 1752 by Maria Theresa's husband for the entertainment and education of the court. Today, it's a modern A (anteater) to Z (zebra) menagerie that's especially appealing to families (€18.50, daily 9:00-18:30, closes earlier off-season, www.zoovienna.at). The Schönbrunn **Imperial Carriage Museum** is a 19th-century traffic jam of 50 impressive Cinderella-style royal carriages and sleighs (€8, daily 9:00-17:00, Nov-April until 16:00, audioguide-€2, 200 yards from palace, walk through right arch as you face palace, tel. 01/525-243-470, www.kaiserliche-wagenburg.at).

Sights in Vienna

A dizzying number of sights and museums cover Vienna's rich culture and vivid history through everything from paintings to music to furniture to prancing horses. To get you started, I've selected the sights that are most essential, rewarding, and user-friendly, and arranged them by neighborhood for handy sightseeing.

When you see a ✪ in a listing, it means the sight is covered in greater detail in my Vienna City Walk or one of my self-guided tours. A ∩ means the walk or tour is also available as a free audio tour (via my Rick Steves Audio Europe app—see page 180).

Bring cash, as some sights don't take credit cards. For more tips on sightseeing, including combo-tickets and sightseeing passes, see page 179.

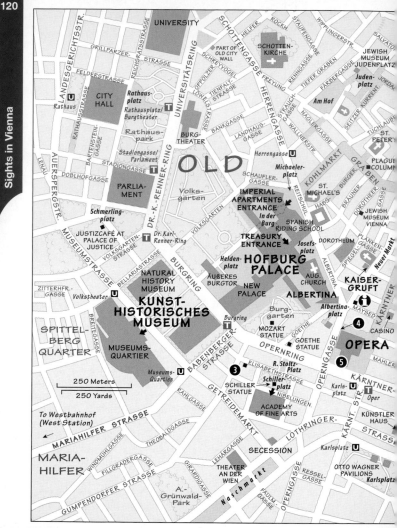

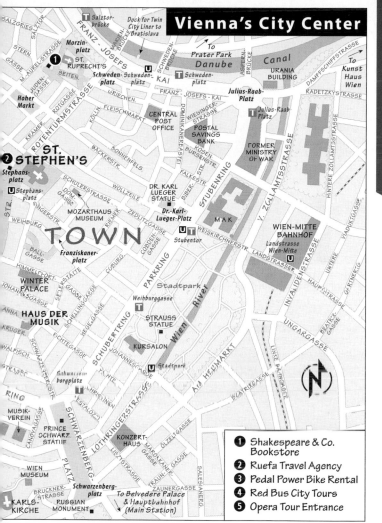

Vienna's City Center

Map labels:

SALZGRIES
SALZTOR-GASSE
STERN GASSE
M. AURELSTRASSE
JUDEN-GASSE
SEITEN
Morzin-platz
ST. RUPRECHT'S
FRANZ-JOSEFS
Salztor-brücke
WEXEN-BRÜCKE
SCHWEDEN-BRÜCKE
Dock for Twin City Liner to Bratislava
To Prater Park
Danube Canal
ASPERN-BRÜCKE
URANIA BUILDING
To Kunst Haus Wien
DAMPFSCHIFFSTRASSE
RADETZKYSTRASSE

Schweden-platz
Schweden-platz
Schweden-platz
KAI
Schweden-platz
Hoher Markt
ROTGASSE
GRIECHEN
FLEISCHMARKT
ZOLL
FRANZ-JOSEFS-KAI
WEISINGER-STRASSE
DOMINIKANERBASTEI
Julius-Raab-Platz
Julius-Raab Platz

KRAMER
ROTENTURMSTRASSE
BÄCKERSTR
CENTRAL POST OFFICE
POSTAL SAVINGS BANK
ROSEN BURGENSTR.
FALKESTR
STUBENRING

ST. STEPHEN'S
Stephans-platz
Stephans-platz
SCHULERSTRASSE
DOM-GASSE
MOZARTHAUS MUSEUM
SINGERSTR
WOLLZEILE
SONNENFELS.
BIBER STR.
DR. KARL LUEGER STATUE
Dr.-Karl-Lueger-Platz
MAK
V. ZOLLAMTSSTRASSE
FORMER MINISTRY OF WAR
HINTERE ZOLLAMTSGASSE
VLADIKAGASSE

WEIHBURG
TOWN
STR
BALL GASSE
Franziskaner-platz
REIMER
ZEDLITZGASSE
CÖBURG
COBDEN GASSE
WEISKIRCHNERSTR.
Stubentor
LANDSTRASSER
WIEN-MITTE BAHNHOF
Landstrasse Wien-Mitte

HIMMELPFORT
WINTER PALACE
JOHANNESGASSE
ANNA
HAUS DER MUSIK
KRUGER
WALFISCH
STRASSE
SEILERSTATTE
SCHELLINGGASSE
HEGELGASSE
RICHTEGASSE
SCHWARZE GASSE
SCHUBERTRING
JOHANNESGASSE
COBURG
CÖBURG
PARKRING
Weihburggasse
Stadtpark
STRAUSS STATUE
KURSALON
Stadtpark
Wien River
Am HEUMARKT
UNGARGASSE
INVALIDENSTRASSE
UNTERE
HAUPTSTRASSE
BEATRIX GASSE
GERINERG
LINKE BAHNGASSE

RING
MUSIK-VEREIN
PRINCE SCHWARZ STATUE
WIEN MUSEUM
BRUCKNER-STRASSE
KARLS-KIRCHE
CANOVA GASSE
SCHWARZENBERG PLATZ
SCHWARZENBERGSTRASSE
LOTHRINGERSTRASSE
FICHTE
CHRISTINEN
KONZERT-HAUS
LISZTSTRASSE
MAROKKANER GASSE
OLZELTGASSE
TRAUN-GASSE
ZAUNERGASSE
SALESIANERG.
BEATRIXGASSE
Schwarzenberg-platz
RUSSIAN MONUMENT
To Belvedere Palace & Hauptbahnhof (Main Station)

Legend:

1. Shakespeare & Co. Bookstore
2. Ruefa Travel Agency
3. Pedal Power Bike Rental
4. Red Bus City Tours
5. Opera Tour Entrance

Hofburg Palace and Related Sights

▲▲▲Hofburg Palace

The imposing Imperial Palace—the main Habsburg residence for over 600 years—is still home to the Austrian president's office, 5,000 government workers, and several important museums. Of the Hofburg's myriad court-yards and museums, focus on three main sights: the Imperial Apartments, the Treasury, and the museums at the New Palace (Neue Burg). With more time, consider the Spanish Riding School (prancing stallions), Augustinian Church (royal crypt), Burggarten park (with statue of Mozart and butterfly house), or the Albertina Museum (Habsburg art collection).

See the ✪ Hofburg Imperial Apartments Tour chapter and the ✪ Hofburg Treasury Tour chapter.

▲▲Hofburg New Palace Museums
(Sammlungen in der Neuen Burg)

The New Palace (Neue Burg) houses three separate collections. **Arms and Armor** is a killer collection of medieval weapons. In the **Ancient Musical Instruments Collection,** you can see (in the large entry hall) Beethoven's (supposed) clarinet and a strange keyboard perhaps played by Mozart. Browse around to find Leopold Mozart's violin (Room XIII) and a piano owned by Schumann and Brahms (Room XVI). The **Ephesus Museum** has artifacts from that bustling ancient Greek, then Roman city (located on modern-day Turkey's southwest coast). One bronze statue of an athlete is a jigsaw of 234 shattered pieces meticulously put back together. The statue of Artemis is draped with round objects—which may have symbol-ized breasts, eggs, or bulls' testicles.

The Hofburg has many sights and museums.

Follow me to the Vienna Boys' Choir!

▶ €15 ticket covers all three collections plus Kunsthistorisches Museum across the Ring, €20 combo-ticket adds Hofburg Treasury, Wed-Sun 10:00-18:00, closed Mon-Tue, audioguide-€3, almost no tourists, tel. 01/525-240, www.khm.at.

▲Spanish Riding School (Spanische Hofreitschule)

The regal Lipizzaner stallions prance to music under chandeliers in a stately 300-year-old Baroque hall. These horses were bred by Habsburg Archduke Charles, who wanted to create an intelligent breed with a noble gait and Baroque profile. They're born black, fade to gray, and turn a distinctive white in adulthood.

The school offers three ways to see the horses—performances, morning exercises, and guided tours of the stables (check the events list on the school's **website** at www.srs.at; enter your dates under "Event Search"). You can purchase tickets online or at the **box office** (opens at

A portrait of young Beethoven alongside his first clarinet—part of the eclectic New Palace

9:00, located inside the Hofburg—go through the main Hofburg entryway from Michaelerplatz, then turn left into the first passage, tel. 01/533-9031).

Free Peek: Any time of day, you can peek through a big window from the covered passageway along Reitschulgasse and usually see the horses poking their heads out of their stalls.

Performances: The Lipizzaner stallions put on great 80-minute performances nearly year-round (they're off in January and some summer weeks). Performances are generally weekends at 11:00 in spring (Feb-mid-June) and fall (mid-Aug-Dec). Tickets (about €50-160) can sell out months in advance, but standing room (about €25) is usually available day of show.

Morning Exercises: Horses and riders trot around to music on weekday mornings in the same hall (€15, generally Tue-Fri 10:00-12:00, no exercises mid-June-July). Enter at Josefsplatz (the large courtyard between Michaelerplatz and Albertinaplatz) at the door marked *Spanische Hofreitschule*). It rarely sells out.

Guided Tours: One-hour tours of the school and stables leave several times almost every afternoon year-round (€18).

▲Augustinian Church (Augustinerkirche)

Built into the Hofburg, this is the Gothic and Neo-Gothic church where the Habsburgs got latched and dispatched (married and buried). Inside (above the altar on the right), notice the windows from which royals witnessed Mass in private. Don't miss the exquisite, pyramid-shaped memorial (by Italian sculptor Antonio Canova) to Maria Theresa's favorite daughter, Maria Christina. The hearts of 54 Habsburg nobles are in urns in a vault off the Loreto Chapel—but they're only accessible to tourists on Sundays after Mass (at about 12:45, €2.50 suggested donation). The church's 11:00 Sunday service is a hit with music lovers—often with a full choir and orchestra playing a Mozart or Haydn Mass (see the program at www.hochamt.at).

▶ *Free, open long hours daily, Augustinerstrasse 3.*

▲▲Albertina Museum

This impressive museum has three highlights: the imposing state rooms *(Prunkräume)* of the former palace, noteworthy collections of classic modernist paintings and European graphic arts, and excellent temporary exhibits. The building, at the southern tip of the Hofburg complex (near the opera), was the residence of Maria Theresa's favorite daughter, Maria Christina.

State Rooms (level 1): Wander freely under chandeliers and across

The Albertina—from Renoir...

...to Picasso and beyond

parquet floors through a handful of rooms of imperial splendor, each a different shade of red, yellow, or green. Most impressive is the large Hall of Muses (in pastel lavender and yellow), lined with statues of the graceful demi-goddesses (plus Apollo) who inspire the arts.

Batliner Collection (level 2): This manageable collection sweeps you quickly through modern art history, featuring minor works by major artists. You'll see classic Impressionism: Monet's water lilies, Degas' dancers, Renoir's cute little girls, and Klimt's eerie femme fatales. The next rooms show the transition from Impressionism to abstraction: the bright colors of Fauvism, and the thick paint and grotesque figures of Expressionism.

The Picasso room has canvases from various periods of his life: early Cubist experiments, portraits of the women in his life, and exuberant colorful works from his last years on the sunny Riviera. Surrealism, paintings by Francis Bacon, and big Abstract Expressionist canvases bring art up to the cusp of the 21st century.

▸ €13, daily 10:00-18:00, Wed until 21:00, helpful audioguide €4, overlooking Albertinaplatz across from the TI and opera, tel. 01/534-830, www.albertina.at.

▲▲Kaisergruft (Imperial Crypt)

Visiting the imperial remains of the Habsburg family is not as easy as you might imagine. These original organ donors left their bodies—about 150 in all—in the unassuming Kaisergruft, their hearts in the Augustinian Church, and their entrails in the crypt below St. Stephen's Cathedral.

Descend into a low-ceilinged crypt full of gray metal tombs. Start up the path, through simple caskets to increasingly big monuments, to the massive pewter tomb of **Maria Theresa** under the dome. The only female

Maria Theresa and her husband relax atop their enormous tomb in the Kaisergruft.

Habsburg monarch, she reigned for 40 enlightened years. She and her husband, **Franz I,** recline atop their fancy coffin, gazing into each other's eyes as a cherub crowns them with glory. At his parents' feet lies **Josef II,** the patron of Mozart and Beethoven.

Continuing to the right of Maria Theresa's tomb, you'll pass the tombs of **Franz II** and his son **Ferdinand I.** These two rulers were forced to relinquish some of the Habsburg power in the face of Napoleon's armies and democratic revolutions.

Through the next room and down three steps, find the tombs of the long-reigning **Franz Josef,** his wife **Elisabeth** (Sisi), and their son, Crown Prince **Rudolf.** In the final room stands a bust (not tomb) of **Karl I**—the final Habsburg ruler, deposed in 1918. When his son, Crown Prince **Otto,** was laid to rest here in 2011, it was probably the last great Old Regime event in European history.

▸ *€5.50, daily 10:00-18:00, €0.50 map includes Habsburg family tree and a chart locating each coffin, crypt is in the Capuchin Church at Tegetthoffstrasse 2 at Neuer Markt; tel. 01/512-6853.*

▲St. Michael's Church Crypt (Michaelerkirche)

St. Michael's Church offers a striking contrast to the imperial crypt. Regular tours take visitors underground to see a typical church crypt, filled with the rotting wooden coffins of well-to-do commoners. You'll meet a 1769 mummy in lederhosen and a wig, along with a woman who is clutching a cross and has flowers painted on her high heels.

▶ €7 for 45-minute tour, Mon-Sat at 11:00 and 13:00, none Sun, enough English, meet at church entrance and pay guide directly, on Michaelerplatz across from Spanish Riding School, mobile 0650-533-8003, www.michaelerkirche.at.

More Sights Within the Ring

▲▲▲St. Stephen's Cathedral (Stephansdom)

This massive Gothic church with the skyscraping spire sits at the center of Vienna. Its highlights are the impressive exterior, the view from the top of the south tower, a carved pulpit, and a handful of quirky sights associated with Mozart and the Habsburg rulers.

😊 See the St. Stephen's Cathedral Tour chapter.

▲▲▲Vienna State Opera (Wiener Staatsoper)

Vienna remains one of the world's great cities for classical music, and this building still belts out some of the finest opera, both classic and cutting edge.

The only way to see the opera house interior (besides attending a performance—see page 185) is with a guided 45-minute tour. You'll see the opulent halls where operagoers gather at intermission, enjoying elaborate spaces with coffered ceilings, gold trim, and ironwork lamps. The highlight is the 2,000-seat theater itself—where the main floor is ringed by box seating, under a huge sugar-doughnut chandelier.

To take a tour, just show up at the tour entrance (southwest corner of the building) 20 minutes beforehand—they don't sell out.

▶ €7.50 for tour, generally run year-round, on the hour from 10:00 to 15:00, fewer tours Sept-June and Sun—check the monthly schedule online, in the opera's monthly Prolog magazine, or posted at the tour entrance; tel. 01/514-442-606, www.wiener-staatsoper.at.

😊 See the Vienna City Walk chapter.

▲▲Haus der Musik

Vienna's "House of Music" is a high-tech experience that celebrates this hometown forte. One floor is dedicated to the heavyweight Viennese composers (Mozart, Beethoven, and company) who virtually created classical music as we know it. Other exhibits use touchscreen computers and headphones to explore the physics of sound. It's open late and is so interactive, relaxing, and fun that it can be considered an activity more than a sight—an evening of joy for music lovers.

▸ *€13, includes app for added info as you visit, half-price after 20:00, €18 combo-ticket with Mozarthaus, daily 10:00-22:00, two blocks from opera house at Seilerstätte 30, tel. 01/513-4850, www.hdm.at.*

▲Dorotheum Auction House (Palais Dorotheum)

Austria's answer to Sotheby's is open to the public to browse (or buy) precious antiques priced for upcoming auctions. There are shops and an info desk with an auction schedule. Back outside, the nearby streets are lined with antique shops.

▸ *Free, Mon-Fri 10:00-18:00, Sat 9:00-17:00, closed Sun, classy café, off the Graben at Dorotheergasse 17, tel. 01/51560, www.dorotheum.com.*

▲St. Peter's Church (Peterskirche)

Baroque Vienna is at its best in this architectural gem, just off the Graben. Admire the rose-and-gold, oval-shaped Baroque interior, topped with a ceiling fresco of Mary kneeling to be crowned by Jesus and the Father, while the dove of the Holy Spirit floats way up in the lantern. The church's sumptuous elements—organ, altar painting, pulpit, and coat of arms—make St. Peter's

Tour the opera house, no reservation needed.

Conduct a virtual band at Haus der Musik.

one of the city's most beautiful and ornate churches. On either side of the nave, glass cases contain skeletons of Christian martyrs from Roman times.

▶ *Free, Mon-Fri 7:00-20:00, Sat-Sun 9:00-21:00; free organ concerts Mon-Fri at 15:00, Sat-Sun at 20:00; just off the Graben between the Plague Monument and Kohlmarkt; tel. 01/533-6433, www.peterskirche.al.*

Mozarthaus Vienna Museum

In September 1784, 27-year-old Wolfgang Amadeus Mozart moved into this spacious apartment with his wife, Constanze, and their week-old son Karl. For the next three years, this was the epicenter of Viennese high life. It was here that Mozart wrote *Marriage of Figaro* and *Don Giovanni* and established himself as the toast of Vienna. Today, the actual apartments are pretty boring (mostly bare rooms), but the museum does flesh out Mozart's Vienna years with paintings, videos, and a few period pieces.

▶ *€11, includes audioguide, €18 combo-ticket with Haus der Musik, daily 10:00-19:00, a block behind the cathedral, go through arcade at #5a and walk 50 yards to Domgasse 5, tel. 01/512-1791, www.mozarthausvienna.at.*

Museum District

▲▲▲Kunsthistorisches Museum

This exciting museum showcases the grandeur and opulence of the Habsburgs' collected artworks in a grand building. You will find world-class European masterpieces galore (including canvases by Raphael, Caravaggio, Velázquez, Vermeer, Rembrandt, and Bruegel).

✪ See the Kunsthistorisches Museum Tour chapter.

▲▲Natural History Museum (Naturhistorisches Museum)

The museum still serves the exact purpose for which it was built: to show off the Habsburgs' vast collection of plant, animal, and mineral specimens and artifacts. It's grown to become an exceptionally well-organized and enjoyable catalogue of the natural world, with 20 million objects, including moon rocks, dinosaur stuff, and the fist-sized *Venus of Willendorf* (at 25,000 years old, the world's oldest sex symbol). Even though the museum has kept its old-school charm, nearly everything on display is presented and described well enough to engage any visitor.

▶ *€10, Wed 9:00-21:00, Thu-Mon 9:00-18:30, closed Tue, on the*

This tiny statue of an ample woman (in the Natural History Museum) is older than the pyramids.

Karlsplatz has Wagner pavilions and a huge church.

Ringstrasse at Maria-Theresien-Platz, U: Volkstheater/Museumsplatz, tel. 01/521-770, www.nhm-wien.ac.at.

MuseumsQuartier

The vast grounds of the former imperial stables now corral a cutting-edge cultural center for contemporary arts and design. Among several impressive museums, the best are the Leopold Museum (Egon Schiele, a few Klimts, and temporary exhibits) and the Museum of Modern Art (a.k.a. MUMOK, with 20th-century "classics" plus contemporary art). For many, the MuseumsQuartier is most enjoyable as a gathering spot in the evening for light, fun meals and cocktails.

▶ *The main entrance/visitors center (www.mqw.at) is at Museumsplatz 1. Check out the museums from their websites (www.leopoldmuseum.org, www.mumok.at).*

Karlsplatz and Nearby

Several of these sights cluster around Karlsplatz, just southeast of the Ringstrasse (U: Karlsplatz). If you're walking from central Vienna, use the U-Bahn station's passageway (at the opera house) to avoid crossing busy boulevards. Once at Karlsplatz, allow about 30 minutes walking time to connect the various sights: Karlskirche, the Secession, and Naschmarkt.

The vast square itself features a Henry Moore sculpture, some green-white-gold pavilions by the Jugendstil pioneer Otto Wagner, and the underappreciated Wien Museum Karlsplatz (www.wienmuseum.at) on the history of Vienna.

▲Karlskirche (St. Charles' Church)

The church, with its massive dome, is dedicated to Charles Borromeo, a bishop who saw Vienna through a 1713 epidemic. The exterior is classic Baroque, with a pediment, 235-foot elliptical dome, and twin spiral columns depicting Borromeo's life.

Inside, gaze up into the dome's colorful 13,500-square-foot fresco, painted in the 1730s by Johann Michael Rottmayr. There, Signor Borromeo (in red-and-white bishops' robes) gazes up into heaven, spreading his arms wide, and pleading with Christ to spare Vienna from the plague.

Ride the elevator (installed for renovation work) up to the base of the dome, then climb sweaty stairs to the tippy-top. At that dizzying height, you're in the clouds among angels and nipple-lipped cupids.

▶ €8, Mon-Sat 9:00-18:00, Sun 13:00-19:00, dome elevator runs until 17:30, audioguide-€2, church hosts concerts, www.karlskirche.at.

▲Academy of Fine Arts Painting Gallery
(Akademie der Bildenden Künste Gemäldegalerie)

Few tourists make their way to Vienna's art academy to see its small but impressive collection of paintings, starring Botticelli, Guardi, Rubens, Van Dyck, and other great masters. The highlight is a triptych by the master of medieval surrealism, Hieronymus Bosch. The collection's location in a working art academy gives it a certain authenticity, and indeed, these paintings were left to the academy for teaching purposes.

▶ €8, Tue-Sun 10:00-18:00, closed Mon; Schillerplatz 3—the painting

Anti-Lutheran fresco in Karlskirche dome

The Karlskirche, with its 235-foot dome

Bosch's surreal triptych is the highlight of the pleasant, quiet, uncrowded Academy of Fine Arts.

gallery is upstairs on the school's first floor, tel. 01/588-162-222, www. akbild.ac.at.

▲The Secession

This little building, strategically located behind the Academy of Fine Arts, was created by the Vienna Secession movement, a group of nonconformist artists led by Gustav Klimt, Otto Wagner, and friends. Having turned their backs on the stuffy official art academy, the Secessionists used the building to display their radical art. The stylized trees carved into the exterior walls and the bushy "golden cabbage" rooftop are symbolic of a cycle of renewal. Today, the Secession continues to showcase contemporary cutting-edge art, and it preserves Gustav Klimt's famous *Beethoven Frieze.* A masterpiece of Viennese Art Nouveau (and inspired by Ludwig van Beethoven's *Ninth Symphony*), this 105-foot-long fresco was the multimedia centerpiece of a 1902 exhibition honoring the composer.

▶ *€9.50 includes special exhibits, Tue-Sun 10:00-18:00, closed Mon, audioguide-€3, Friedrichstrasse 12, tel. 01/587-5307, www.secession.at.*

▲Naschmarkt

This long, wide square is lined with lively produce stalls, shops, and cafés.

The culmination of Klimt's *Beethoven Frieze*: a heavenly choir serenades two lovers

The Naschmarkt (roughly, "Nibble Market") has two parallel lanes—one lined with fun and reasonable eateries, the other featuring top-end produce and gourmet goodies. Vienna's top chefs shop here. At the gourmet vinegar stall, you can sample the vinegar as you would perfume—with a drop on your wrist. Farther from the center, the Naschmarkt becomes likably seedy, less expensive, and surrounded by sausage stands, Turkish *döner kebab* stalls, and cafés. Each Saturday, the Naschmarkt is infested by a huge flea market (west of the Kettenbrückengasse U-Bahn station). Picnickers can pick up their grub in the market and head over to Karlsplatz or the Burggarten.

▶ *Mon-Fri 6:00-18.30, Sat until 17:00, closed Sun, closes earlier in winter; between Linke Wienzeile and Rechte Wienzeile, U: Karlsplatz.*

Museums Beyond the Ring

▲▲Belvedere Palace (Schloss Belvedere)

This is the elegant palace of Prince Eugene of Savoy (1663-1736), the still much-appreciated conqueror of the Ottomans. Eugene, a Frenchman considered too short and too ugly to be in the service of Louis XIV, instead served the Habsburgs, becoming the savior of Austria and the toast of Viennese society.

Today you can tour Eugene's lavish palace, see sweeping views of the gardens and the Vienna skyline, and enjoy world-class art starring Gustav Klimt, French Impressionism, and a grab bag of other 19th- and early 20th-century artists.

The Naschmarkt is perfect for strolling, noshing, drinking, and people watching.

Focus on the Upper Palace, where the major art is. From the entrance, climb the staircase to the first floor and enter a grand red-and-gold, chandeliered room.

Marble Hall: This was Prince Eugene's party room. The ceiling fresco shows Eugene (in the center, wearing blue and pink) about to be crowned with a laurel wreath. *Belvedere* means "beautiful view," and the view from the Marble Hall is especially spectacular: Look over the Baroque gardens and Lower Palace to the city. Find the green dome of St. Peter's Church and the spire of St. Stephen's (where Eugene is buried, see page 41). The hills beyond—covered with vineyards—are where the Viennese go to sample new wine (see page 141).

East Wing: Pass by Renoir's ladies, Monet's landscapes, and Van Gogh's rough brushstrokes to find two rooms dedicated to Vienna's master of Modernism—**Gustav Klimt.** You can get caught up in his fascination with the beauty and danger he saw in women. His *Judith* (1901) is no biblical heroine—she's a high-society Viennese woman with an ostentatious dog-collar necklace. With half-closed eyes and slightly parted lips, she's bewitching. Holding the head of her victim, she's the modern femme fatale. In *The Kiss,* two lovers are wrapped up in the colorful gold-and-jeweled cloak of bliss. The man is Klimt himself. Klimt nurtured the next generation of artists, especially **Egon Schiele,** whose works (like the darker and more introspective *Embrace*) hang nearby.

The Rest of the Upper Palace: The Belvedere's collection goes through the whole range of 19th- and 20th-century art: Historicism, Romanticism, Impressionism, Realism, tired tourism, Expressionism, Art Nouveau, and early Modernism. In the west wing of the **first floor** is the Belvedere's collection of Austrian Baroque art, and back on the **main floor** are Expressionist works from between the world wars and medieval art. The **second floor** up shows off early-19th-century paintings in the Biedermeier style.

Gardens: The delightfully manicured grounds are free and fun to explore. The Lower Palace (temporary exhibits) requires an entry fee.

▸ *€14 for Upper Belvedere Palace only, €20 for Upper and Lower Palaces (and special exhibits), gardens free; daily 10:00-18:00; Lower Palace until 21:00 on Wed, grounds open until dusk, audioguide €4, charming café; entrance at Prinz-Eugen-Strasse 27, tel. 01/7955-7134, www.belvedere.at.*

The palace is a 15-minute walk south of the Ring. Or take tram #D from the opera house (direction: Hauptbahnhof) to the Schloss Belvedere stop. Cross the street, walk uphill one block, go left through the gate, and look right for the small ticket office.

▲Kunst Haus Wien Museum and Hundertwasserhaus

This museum and nearby apartment complex are a hit with lovers of modern art, mixing the work and philosophy of local painter/environmentalist Friedensreich Hundertwasser (1928-2000)—a.k.a. "1001 I2O."

Belvedere Palace: Gardens, views, and...   ...fine art, starring Klimt's *The Kiss*

Jugendstil and the Vienna Secession

As Europe approached the dawn of a new (nouveau) century, artists began creating a truly new and free art style that left behind the stodginess of the 19th century. Though the Art Nouveau movement began in Paris and Belgium, each country gave it its own spin. In German-speaking lands, Art Nouveau was called Jugendstil—"youth style."

Art Nouveau was forward-looking, embracing the new technology of iron and glass. But it was also a reaction against the sheer ugliness of the mass-produced, boxy Industrial Age. Art Nouveau artists embraced nature and the sinuous curves of organic plant forms. Art Nouveau street lamps twist and bend like flower stems, and ironwork fountains sprout buds that squirt water. Art Nouveau was a total "look" that could be applied to furniture, jewelry, paintings, and even entire buildings.

Vienna's Art Nouveau/Jugendstil movement is called "The Secession." Gustav Klimt, Otto Wagner, Egon Schiele, Oskar Kokoschka, and others disdained the prevailing art styles of the 19th century, and dared to "secede" from conventionalism. The Secessionist motto was: "To each age its art, and to art its liberty."

Of the two sights here designed by Hundertwasser—the museum and the *haus* itself—the museum is best. Admire the museum's jaunty checkerboard exterior and lush greenery. Inside, you'll learn about the man's life and art, peppered with his colorful quotes.

A 5- to 10-minute walk takes you to Hundertwasserhaus (at Löwengasse and Kegelgasse). This complex of 50 apartments was built in the 1980s as a breath of architectural fresh air in a city of boring, blocky apartments. While not open to visitors, it's worth seeing for its fun and colorful patchwork exterior and the Hundertwasser festival of shops across the street. Don't miss the view from Kegelgasse to see the "tree tenants" and the internal winter garden that residents enjoy.

The Hundertwasserhaus complex shows this unique designer's love of color and curvy lines.

▶ *€11 for museum, more for special exhibits, daily 10:00-18:00, extremely fragrant and colorful garden café, tel. 01/712-0491, www.kunsthauswien.com.*

The museum is located at Untere Weissgerberstrasse 13, near the Radetzkyplatz stop on trams #O and #1 (signs point the way). Take the U-Bahn to Landstrasse and walk 10 minutes downhill (north) along Untere Viaduktgasse or transfer to tram #O (direction: Praterstern) and ride three stops to Radetzkyplatz.

Sigmund Freud Museum

Freud enthusiasts enjoy seeing the apartment and home office of the man who fundamentally changed our understanding of the human psyche. Dr. Sigmund Freud (1856-1939), a graduate of Vienna University, spent 47 years at this office, receiving troubled patients who hoped to find peace by telling him their dreams, life traumas, and secret urges. It was here that he wrote his landmark *Interpretation of Dreams* (1899). You can see Freud's cane, hat, pocket flask, and collection of primitive fertility figurines. Old photos and documents trace his fascinating (if Vienna-centric) life. What you won't see is his famous couch: He took that with him when he fled the Nazis.

▶ *€10, includes audioguide, daily 10:00-18:00, tiny bookshop, half-block from Schlickgasse stop on tram #D, Berggasse 19, tel. 01/319-1596, www.freud-museum.at. For location, see map on page 53.*

▲Imperial Furniture Collection (Hofmobiliendepot)

Bizarre, sensuous, eccentric, or precious, this extensive collection is your peek at the Habsburgs' furniture—from the empress's wheelchair ("to increase her fertility she was put on a rich diet and became corpulent") to the emperor's spittoon—all thoughtfully described in English. Evocative

The Freud Museum has the office of…

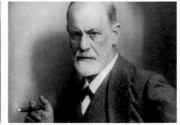
Sigmund Freud, a Vienna native.

paintings help bring the furniture to life. When the Habsburgs moved from palace to palace, they had roadies to bring their furniture with them.

▶ *€9.50, covered by Sisi Ticket (see page 180), Tue-Sun 10:00-18:00, closed Mon, Mariahilfer Strasse 88, main entrance around the corner at Andreas-gasse 7, U: Zieglergasse, tel. 01/5243-3570, www.hofmobiliendepot.at.*

On Vienna's Outskirts

▲▲▲Schönbrunn Palace (Schloss Schönbrunn)
The summer home of the Habsburgs, this is one of Europe's great Baroque palaces, featuring opulent rooms, history of its famous occupants, and the wander-perfect gardens.

⭘ See the Schönbrunn Palace Tour chapter.

▲Prater Park (Wiener Prater)
Since the 1780s, this place has been Vienna's playground. For the tourist, the "Prater" is the sugary-smelling and sprawling amusement park

Prater Park—low-brow fun with locals

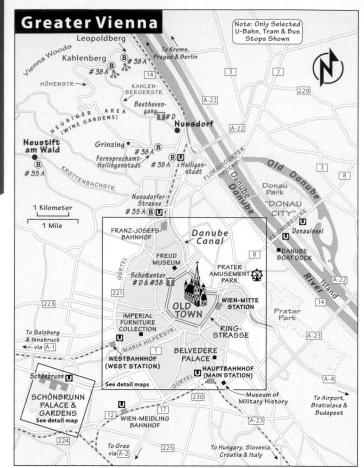

Greater Vienna

Note: Only Selected
U-Bahn, Tram & Bus
Stops Shown

Leopoldberg

To Krems, Prague & Berlin

Vienna Woods

Kahlenberg

B #38A

B #38A

HÖHENSTR.

KAHLEN-
BERGERSTR.

A-22

Beethoven-
gang

T #D

Nussdorf

A-22

HEURIGER AREA
(WINE GARDENS)

Neustift
am Wald

B

#35A

Grinzing

Fernsprechamt-
Heiligenstadt

#38A B

#38A

B U Heiligen-
stadt

FLORIDSDORFER BRÜCKE

Danube

Danube

Old Danube

Donau
Park

"DONAU
CITY"

3

8

KROTTENBACHSTR.

Nussdorfer-
Strasse

#35A B U

REICHSBRÜCKE

Donauinsel

1 Kilometer

1 Mile

FRANZ-JOSEFS-
BAHNHOF

GÜRTEL

Danube
Canal

FREUD
MUSEUM

Schottentor
#D & #38

221

IMPERIAL
FURNITURE
COLLECTION

223

To Salzburg
& Innsbruck
via A-1

Schönbrunn U

SCHÖNBRUNN
PALACE &
GARDENS
See detail map

224

MARIA HILFERSTR.

U

WESTBAHNHOF
(WEST STATION)

1

OLD
TOWN

PRATER
AMUSEMENT
PARK

8

DANUBE
BOAT DOCK

Island

A-22

River

14

WIEN-MITTE
STATION

RING-
STRASSE

Prater
Park

A-23

BELVEDERE
PALACE

GÜRTEL

U HAUPTBAHNHOF
(MAIN STATION)

A-4

See detail maps

12 U

WIEN-MEIDLING
BAHNHOF

17

230

Museum of
Military History

To Airport,
Bratislava &
Budapest

A-23

225

To Graz
via A-2

To Hungary, Slovenia,
Croatia & Italy

(Wurstelprater). For locals, the "Prater" is the vast, adjacent green park with its three-mile-long, tree-lined main boulevard (Hauptallee). The park still tempts visitors with its famous 220-foot-tall Ferris wheel, roller coasters, bumper cars, Lilliputian railroad, and endless eateries. Especially if you're traveling with kids, this is a fun place to share the evening with thousands of Viennese.

▶ *Park is free and always open, amusement park—rides cost €2-€8 and run May-Oct roughly 10:00-22:00, but often later in good weather in summer, fewer rides open in off-season, U: Praterstern, www.prater.at. For a local-style family dinner, eat at Schweizerhaus (good food, great Czech Budvar—the original "Budweiser"—beer, classic conviviality).*

A Walk in the Vienna Woods (Wienerwald)
For a quick side-trip into the woods and out of the city, catch the U-4 subway line to Heiligenstadt, then bus #38A to Kahlenberg, where you'll enjoy great views and a café overlooking the city. From there, it's a peaceful 45-minute downhill hike to the *Heurigen* of Nussdorf or to enjoy some new wine (see next listing).

Wein in Wien: Vienna's Wine Gardens
Sipping wine on a balmy evening under a leafy canopy, surrounded by the very vineyards that produced it—it's a typically Viennese experience. A *Heuriger* (HOY-rih-gur)—the wine equivalent of a beer garden—lets you enjoy wines by the glass and food from a buffet, in a pleasant atmosphere, indoors or out. These wine gardens are named for their specialty: the new wine *(heurig)* that vintners break out every November 11 and serve for the following 365 days. Many *Heurigen* are decorated with draped vines and antique presses, and some have live (traditional) music or play zones for kids.

The experience is best in good weather and lively weekends, but you can eat indoors too. Most *Heurigen* open up in the afternoon (generally between 14:00 and 16:00) and close late (about 24:00, but some are closed or have earlier hours Sundays and Mondays, and some close completely in mid-winter.

Before going anywhere, remember there's a pretty good *Heuriger* right in the city center: **Gigerl Stadtheuriger** (see page 159). But it's surprisingly easy and rewarding to leave the city, away from the tourist crowds and into a slower-paced world.

Getting There: I recommend the neighborhood of Nussdorf/ Heiligenstadt, 30 minutes north of downtown on the tram (or a 15-minute, €20 taxi). Take tram #D from the Ringstrasse to its endpoint, the Beethovengang stop (despite what it says on the front of the tram, the Nussdorf stop isn't the end—stay on for one more stop). (See Tram #D on the map on page 176.) This puts you in Nussdorf, a working-class neighborhood of real shops and real locals. Cross the tram tracks and find the back entrance to the **Schübel-Auer Heuriger,** my favorite wine-garden here. It offers a big and user-friendly buffet, and its rustic ambience can be enjoyed indoors or out (opens at 16:00, closed Sun-Mon and mid-Dec-mid-Feb, Kahlenberger Strasse 22, tel. 01/370-2222). Next door is **Heuriger Kierlinger** (opens at 15:30, closed most of August and periodically in off-season, Kahlenberger Strasse 20, tel. 01/370-2264).

For still more atmosphere, ask a local to point you to "Pfarrplatz," a 5- to 10-minute walk away. This square anchors the quaint village of Heiligenstadt, where Beethoven worked on his Ninth Symphony. Enjoy the vine-draped, famous-but-touristy **Mayer am Pfarrplatz** (opens

Drink with locals at a *Heurigen* wine garden.

A Page of History

Vienna is a head without a body—the capital of the once-great Habsburg empire. Vienna sits at the "crossroads of Europe," where the west-east Danube River crosses the north-south route through the Alps. Charlemagne (c. 800) made Austria one edge of his European empire—the "Eastern Realm," or *Österreich*.

Charlemagne's title of Holy Roman Emperor was bestowed upon Rudolf I (1273), the first Habsburg to carry the title. The family would rule Austria for the next six centuries. Under Emperor Frederick III (c. 1450)—the "father" of Vienna—the city became a cosmopolitan capital. By the time of Charles V (r. 1519-1556), the Habsburgs controlled the world's largest empire.

Over the years, the Habsburgs struggled against Protestant reformers, bubonic plague (1679), Ottoman Turks (1683 siege), and wars with Louis XIV of France (1672-1714). Maria Theresa (c. 1750) bolstered Austria's prestige by marrying off her 16 kids to Europe's royalty. Under her son Josef II, Vienna enjoyed a renaissance of music—Mozart, Haydn, Beethoven.

Napoleon's revolutionaries defeated Austria (1805), but after Napoleon's defeat at Waterloo, Vienna hosted the congress (1815) that reinstalled Europe's conservative monarchies.

By 1850, Vienna was the epicenter of European culture: fine music, coffee, chocolates, and dress-up balls; a city of scientists (Doppler), thinkers (Freud), and artists (Klimt). The old city wall was torn down to become the Ringstrasse. As the century turned, Vienna teetered between Old World elegance and subversive modernism. Revolutionaries demanded freedom, and the world was industrializing and globalizing.

In 1914, the Habsburg heir was assassinated, sparking World War I. By war's end, the Habsburg empire was dissolved, with Austria's borders reduced to those it has today. In the run-up to World War II, Austrian fascists gained power, and Nazi Germany annexed the country (1938's *Anschluss*). Austria suffered the consequences of war: Thousands died in nearby death camps, and half of Vienna was destroyed.

But the city rebuilt. Austria became a democratic nation (1955), a site of summits between Cold War superpowers, and home to several UN organizations. Today, it's a member of the European Union.

at 16:00, Pfarrplatz 2, tel. 01/370-1287) or the more traditional-but-fun **Weingut and Heuriger Werner Welser** (opens at 16:30, Probusgasse 12, tel. 01/318-9797).

To get home, backtrack to Nussdorf and catch Tram #D (last tram around midnight). Or, from Heiligenstadt, catch the frequent bus #38A to the Heiligenstadt U-4 station, where the subway takes you back to town. Or have your wine garden call you a taxi.

Ordering Food and Drink: In general, you seat yourself, and order and pay for drinks when a waiter comes. An 8-ounce glass of new wine (a *Viertel,* FEER-tehl) costs about €3. *Traubenmost* is nonalcoholic grape juice, *Most* is young and lightly alcoholic, and *Sturm* is older and stronger.

For food, you go to the various buffet counters to choose and pay for the dishes you want; they'll bring your prepared plate to you. You'll find main dishes like ham, roast beef, chicken, roulade, or meatloaf. Side dishes include casseroles, sauerkraut, salads, bread, and cheese. Food is sold by weight—*"10 dag"* is 100 grams, or a quarter-pound. Many vendors speak English, and pointing also works.

Music Sights

For music lovers, Vienna is an opportunity to make pilgrimages to the homes of favorite composers. If you're a fan of Schubert, Brahms, Haydn, Beethoven, or Mozart, there's a sight for you. But I find these homes inconveniently located and generally underwhelming.

Instead, I prefer to tour the opera house (or get standing-room tickets for a performance), take in a concert, attend a musical Sunday Mass at the Augustinian Church, visit the Haus der Musik, or browse the Ancient Musical Instruments Collection in the Hofburg's New Palace. To bring

Young Mozart came of age in Vienna.

The opera sells cheap standing-room tix.

Melk Abbey is just one of the picturesque sights in the nearby Danube Valley.

home top-quality classical CDs, shop at Gramola on the Graben, EMI on Kärntner Strasse, or Arcadia at the Vienna State Opera.

Every January 1, just after midnight, 50 million people around the world welcome the New Year by watching a broadcast of the Vienna Philharmonic playing a waltz by Strauss.

Day Trips (and Beyond)

Melk and the Danube Valley (rustic pastoral beauty) are an hour plus by train. Bratislava (the up-and-coming capital of Slovakia) is an hour by train (or a longer boat ride that's not as scenic as it sounds).

Still farther, Vienna is a good jumping-off point by train for musical Salzburg (3 hours), charming Hallstatt (4 hours), Innsbruck (4.5 hours), Mauthausen Concentration Camp Memorial (2 hours), Budapest, Hungary (2.5 hours), and Prague, Czech Republic (4 hours).

Sleeping

Accommodations in Vienna are plentiful and relatively cheap—a €100 double here might go for €150 in Munich and €200 in Milan. I've grouped my hotel listings into two—well, really three—neighborhoods: The **Old Town** (within the Ring) is most central, atmospheric, and pricey. **Mariahilfer Strasse** (stretching from the Ring to the Westbahnhof) is less classy but a better value, and has two distinct areas: Its **east end** is more gentrified, while the **west end** (near the train station) is rougher.

I like hotels that are clean, central, reasonably priced, friendly, small enough to have a hands-on owner and stable staff, and run with a respect for Austrian traditions. Double rooms listed in this book average around €100 (including a private bathroom). They range from a low of roughly €60 (very simple, with toilet and shower down the hall) to €290 (maximum plumbing and more).

A Typical Vienna Hotel Room

A typical €100 double room in Vienna's city center will be small by American standards. It will have one double bed (either queen-sized or slightly narrower) or two twins. There's probably a bathroom in the room with a toilet, sink, and bathtub or shower. The room has a telephone and TV, and may have a safe. Single rooms, triples, and quads will have similar features.

Some hotels occupy one floor of a building with a finicky vintage elevator or dingy entryway. The hotelier doesn't control the common areas of the building, so try not to let the entryway atmosphere color your opinion of the hotel. Air-conditioning is rare, but fans are usually available. Viennese elevators can be confusing, with letters instead of floor numbers; press "E" for the ground floor. Some hotels still allow smoking, so ask about nonsmoking rooms when you book. The staff speaks English.

Breakfast—often included in the room price—might be as little as bread and coffee, but usually includes a self-serve buffet with cereal, ham, cheese, yogurt, and juice. Most accommodations have free Wi-Fi.

Making Reservations

Reserve your rooms several weeks or even months in advance—or as soon as you've pinned down your travel dates. Expect rates to spike higher for conventions (Sept-Oct), and dip in July and August. The days around New Year's Eve are always busy.

Make reservations by phone, through the hotel's website, or with an email that covers:

- the size of your party and type of rooms you need
- your arrival and departure dates, written European-style—day followed by month and year (for example, 18/06/18 or 18 June 2018); include the total number of nights
- special requests (such as en suite bathroom vs. down the hall, cheapest room, twin beds vs. double bed, quiet room)
- applicable discounts (such as a Rick Steves reader discount, cash discount, or promotional rate)

If they require your credit-card number for a deposit, you can send it by email (I do), but it's safer via phone, the hotel's secure website, or split between two emails. Once your room is booked, print out the confirmation, and reconfirm your reservation with a phone call or email a day or

Hotel Price Code

$$$$	**Splurge:**	Most rooms over €170
$$$	**Pricier:**	€130-170
$$	**Moderate:**	€90-130
$	**Budget:**	€50-90
¢	**Backpacker:**	Under €50
RS%	**Rick Steves discount**	

These rates are for a standard double room with breakfast in high season. For the best prices, book directly with the hotel.

two in advance (alert them if you'll be arriving after 17:00). If canceling a reservation, some hotels require advance notice—otherwise they may bill you. Even if there's no penalty, it's polite to give at least three days' notice.

Budget Tips
To get the best rates, book directly with the hotel, not through a third-party site. Start with the hotel's website, looking for promo deals. Email several hotels to ask for their best price and compare offers. Some may give a discount if you stay at least three nights or pay in cash.

Besides hotels, there are cheaper alternatives. Guesthouses (the Austrian equivalent to B&Bs, called *Pensionen*) offer a personal touch at a fair price—I've listed several. I also list a few all-ages hostels, which offer €25-30 dorm beds (and a few inexpensive doubles) and come with curfews and other rules. Websites such as www.airbnb.com make it reasonably easy to find a place to sleep in someone's home.

Renting an apartment can save money if you're traveling as a family, staying more than a week, and planning to cook your own meals. Try www.homeaway.com (offering a wide range of listings) or www.vrbo.com (putting you directly in touch with owners).

Don't be too cheap when picking a place to stay. Anything under €90 (even my listings) can be a little rough around the edges. Choose a nice, central neighborhood. Consider asking for a quiet room in back. Your Vienna experience will be more memorable with a welcoming oasis to call home.

Sleeping

OLD TOWN: Within the Ringstrasse, walking distance to sights, pricier but more atmospheric—the classiest Vienna experience. U: Stephansplatz or Karlsplatz.

$$$$ Hotel am Stephansplatz Stephansplatz 9 | tel. 01/534-050, www.hotelamstephansplatz.at	Four-star business hotel, plush but modern (air-con, gym), great breakfast, stunning view of cathedral next door
$$$ Pension Aviano Marco d'Avianogasse 1 tel. 01/512-8330, www.secrethomes.at	Peaceful, above the action, family-run, great value, 17 Baroque-frill rooms, RS%
$$$ Motel One Staatsoper Elisabethstrasse 5 tel. 01/585-0505, www.motel-one.com	400 sleek, modern rooms with Old World charm, fantastic lounge spaces
$$$ Hotel Pertschy Habsburgergasse 5 tel. 01/534-490, www.pertschy.com	Circling an old courtyard, 56 huge rooms, elegantly creaky, chandeliers and Baroque touches, courtyard rooms quietest
$$$ Hotel zur Wiener Staatsoper Krugerstrasse 11 | tel. 01/513-1274, www.zurwienerstaatsoper.at	Quiet, traditional elegance, 22 tidy rooms with high ceilings, chandeliers, and fancy carpets on parquet floors
$$$ Pension Nossek Graben 17 | tel. 01/5337-0410, www.pension-nossek.at	Tastefully decorated B&B with lace and flowers, quiet despite location on Graben
$$ Pension A und A Habsburgergasse 3 tel. 01/890-5128, www.aunda.at	Friendly nine-room B&B run by Andreas and Andrea, elegant modern break from crusty old Vienna, near Graben
$$ Pension Suzanne Walfischgasse 4 | tel. 01/513-2507, www.pension-suzanne.at	Baroque and doily antique furnishings, right by opera house, small but run with class, RS%
$$ Schweizer Pension Heinrichsgasse 2 | tel. 01/533-8156, www.schweizerpension.com	Family-run by helpful Anita and son Gerald, 11 homey tidy rooms, four with shared facilities
$$ Pension Neuer Markt Seilergasse 9 tel. 01/512-2316, www.hotelpension.at	Family-run, central, 37 comfy but faded rooms, cool quiet courtyard rooms best in summer
$$ Pension Dr. Geissler Postgasse 14 tel. 01/533-2803, www.hotelpension.at	23 respectable plain-but-comfortable rooms on upper floor of nondescript building off Schwedenplatz

MARIAHILFER STRASSE—EAST: Lively street on convenient U-3 line between Westbahnhof and downtown; inexpensive stores and cafés; best neighborhood for drivers; some prefer cash, others cash-only; east end of the street is more gentrified—closer to downtown and a short walk to the Museum District/Spittelberg and the Naschmarkt. U: Zieglergasse or Neubaugasse.

$$$ NH Collection Wien Zentrum Mariahilfer Strasse 78 tel. 01/524-5600, www.nh-hotels.com	Big, stern chain hotel, stylish but passionless, suites (with kitchenette) are ideal for families
$$ Hotel Kugel Siebensterngasse 43 tel. 01/523-3355, www.hotelkugel.at	Run with pride by gentlemanly Johannes Roller, 25 charming Old World rooms, good family rooms
$$ Haydn Hotel Mariahilfer Strasse 57 tel. 01/587-4140, www.haydn-hotel.at	Formal business hotel with 21 bland, spacious, modern rooms, RS%
$$ Hotel Pension Corvinus Mariahilfer Strasse 57 tel. 01/587/7239, www.corvinus.at	15 bright, comfortable rooms, run by Hungarian Miklós, Judit, Anthony, and Zoltán, family rooms and apartments available
$$ K&T Boardinghouse Chwallagasse 2 | tel. 01/523-2989, mobile 0676-553-6083 www.ktboardinghouse.at	5 spacious rooms on first floor of quiet building a block off Mariahilfer Strasse, no breakfast
$ Hotel Pension Mariahilf Mariahilfer Strasse 49 | tel. 01/586-1781, www.mariahilf-hotel.at	12 good-sized and well-priced (if a bit outmoded) rooms, high ceilings, near U-Bahn
$ Pension Kraml Brauergasse 5 tel. 01/587-8500, www.pensionkraml.at	17 big, charming Old World rooms on small quiet street, family-run, stairs, no elevator
$ Pension Hargita Andreasgasse 1 tel. 01/526-1928, www.hargita.at	24 bright, attractive rooms (mostly twins) with woody Hungarian-village decor, on busy street but still quiet

MARIAHILFER STRASSE—WEST: Near the Westbahnhof, these hotels (and several hostels) offer the same convenient U-Bahn connection to downtown, but they're generally less atmospheric and in a rougher neighborhood. U: Westbahnhof.

$$ Motel One Westbahnhof Europaplatz 3 tel. 01/359-350, www.motel-one.com	By the Westbahnhof, huge chain hotel offers low-budget, no-frills business accommodations

$ Hotel Ibis Wien Mariahilf Mariahilfer Gürtel 22 tel. 01/59998, www.ibishotel.com	Big, modern high-rise hotel, bright cookie-cutter rooms, antidote to quaint old Europe
$ Pension Fünfhaus Sperrgasse 12 tel. 01/892-3545, www.pension5haus.at	Plain, clean, bare-bones, and institutional, with 47 great-price rooms in an improving neighborhood
¢ Hostel Ruthensteiner Robert-Hamerling-Gasse 24 tel. 01/893-4202, www.hostelruthensteiner.com	100 beds in 4- to 8-bed dorm rooms, as "cozy" as a hostel can be, some private rooms
¢ Westend City Hostel Fügergasse 3 tel. 01/597-6729, www.westendhostel.at	Hostel a block from Westbahnhof in quieter residential neighborhood, some private rooms
¢ Wombat's City Hostel Mariahilfer Strasse 137 | tel. 01/897-2336, www.wombats-hostels.com	Hostel with 250 beds and some private rooms, generous public spaces, one other location nearby
¢ Hostel Wien Myrthengasse 7 tel. 01/523-6316, hostel@chello.at	Classic, huge, well-run official youth hostel, 260 beds, private rooms available, bus #48A
MORE HOTELS IN VIENNA: If my top listings are full, here are some others to consider.	
$$$ Hotel Domizil Schulerstrasse 14 tel. 01-513-3199, www.hoteldomizil.at	40 rooms that are light, bright, and neat as a pin—and near Stephansplatz
$$$ Hotel Marc Aurel Marc Aurel Strasse 8 | tel. 01-533-5226, www.hotel-marcaurel.com	Affordable, plain-Jane business-class hotel a few steps from Schwedenplatz
$$ Theaterhotel Josefstädter Strasse 22 tel. 01-405-3648, www.cordial.at	Shiny gem of a hotel on a fun shopping street near the City Hall (Rathaus)
$$ Hotel Astoria Kärntner Strasse 32 tel. 01-515-771-00, www.austria-trend.at/hotel-astoria	Turn-of-the-century Old World hotel with 128 classy rooms just off Kärntner Strasse

Eating

The Viennese appreciate the fine points of life, and right up there with waltzing is eating.

The city has many atmospheric restaurants, serving top-notch cuisine tinged with Hungarian and Bohemian flavors. In addition to restaurants, you'll find some uniquely Viennese institutions: the city's café culture and its *Heuriger* wine pubs.

My listings are (mostly) in three atmospheric neighborhoods: First is the **Old Town,** clustered near St. Stephen's, the opera house, and the atmospheric lanes of Am Hof Square. In the **Museum District** (just west of the Ring) are the cobbled lanes of Spittelberg. **Mariahilfer Strasse** (with many recommended hotels) is lined with reasonable cafés serving all types of cuisine.

The Story of Viennese Coffee

The story of coffee in Vienna is steeped in legend. In the 17th century, the Ottomans (invaders from the Turkish Empire) laid siege to Vienna. An Austrian spy infiltrated the Ottoman ranks and got to know the Turkish lifestyle...including their passion for a drug called coffee. After the Austrians persevered, the ecstatic Habsburg emperor offered the spy anything he wanted. The spy asked for the Ottomans' spilled coffee beans, which he gathered up to start the first coffee shop in town. (Or so goes the over-caffeinated legend.)

No matter where you dine, expect it to be *gemütlich*—a much-prized Austrian virtue meaning an atmosphere of relaxed coziness.

When in Vienna...

I eat on the Austrian schedule. For breakfast, I eat at the hotel (fresh-baked bread, meat, cheese, cereal) or grab a pastry and coffee at a café. Traditionally, the Austrian lunch (12:00-14:00) is a big meal (many restaurants offer dinner-size lunch specials), though health-conscious Viennese of today may choose lighter fare. In between meals, I might stop at a takeout stand for a wurst. In the late afternoon, the Viennese enjoy a beverage with friends at an outdoor table on a lively square. Dinner (18:00-21:00) is the time for slowing down and savoring a multi-course restaurant meal.

Restaurant Etiquette

Full-service, sit-down restaurants in Austria operate much like restaurants everywhere, but there are a few small differences in etiquette.

Tipping is not necessary (because a service charge is usually included in the menu price), but a tip of about 5-10 percent is a nice reward for good service. Give the tip directly to your server. Austrians prefer not leaving coins on the table. So, for a €10 meal, they might tip €1 by paying with a €20 bill and telling the waiter the total they wish to pay: *"Elf, bitte"*—"Eleven, please"—to get €9 change.

Main dishes don't automatically come with side dishes. Austrians are willing to pay for bottled water with their meal (*Mineralwasser mit/ohne*

Gas—with/without carbonation), and tap water *(Leitungswasser)* may cost around €0.50. You might be charged for bread you've eaten from the basket on the table; have the waiter take it away if you don't want it. Some (pricier) restaurants have a small cover charge. Most restaurants are closed Sunday. Many Austrian eateries still have a smoking section, so even the nonsmoking section may have secondhand smoke.

Many places offer pleasant outdoor seating in good weather; there's usually no extra charge to sit outside. Most restaurants offer a *"menu"*—a fixed-price meal—at lunchtime on weekdays (typically around €10 for a main course plus soup or salad). The best dish on any menu is often the house specialty. For smaller portions, order from the *kleine Hunger* (small hunger) section of the menu.

Good service is relaxed service—only a rude waiter will rush you. When you want the bill, say, *"Rechnung* (REKH-nung), *bitte."* To wish others "Happy eating!" offer a cheery *"Guten Appetit!"*

Cafés, *Beisls*, and More

Besides fancy restaurants, there are other less-formal places to fill the tank.

Other Restaurants: I love *Beisls.* A *Beisl* (BYE-zul) is a neighborhood pub that serves hearty food and drinks at an affordable price. Ask your hotel to recommend a good *Beisl.* (Some are smoky, but most have outdoor seating.) Ethnic restaurants are popular, especially Asian, Turkish (good values), and Italian. Hotels often serve fine food. A *Gaststatte* is just a simple, less-expensive restaurant.

Cheap Takeout Meals and Picnics: Vienna makes it easy to turn a picnic into a first-class affair. Grab something to go and enjoy a bench in a lively square or leafy park. It's easy to find sandwiches and boxed salads at bakeries, delis, and supermarkets; try *Wurstsemmel* (a sausage sandwich) or *Schnitzelsemmel* (a schnitzel sandwich). Other cheap eateries include department-store cafeterias and *Schnellimbiss* (fast-food) stands. *Döner kebab* kiosks serve shaved meat and vegetables wrapped in pita bread.

Best of the Wurst: In Austria, you're never far from a *Würstelstand* (sausage stand). The *wurst,* usually pork sausage, comes in many varieties. *Bratwurst* is a generic term that simply means "grilled sausage." A *Burenwurst* is what we'd call "kielbasa." There's also *Bockwurst, Weisswurst, Liverwurst,* and so on. Generally, the darker the weenie, the spicier it is.

Dine in a woodsy medieval interior...

...or outside, usually at no extra charge.

Your *wurst* comes on a paper plate with your choice of bread *(Brot)* or roll *(Semmel),* and with ketchup or mustard—sweet *(süss)* or sharp *(scharf).* Locals don't put the sausage in the bread like a hot dog. They take a bite of sausage, then a bite of bread. ("That's why you have two hands.")

Americans call their plain sausages a *Wiener* after the city of Vienna—a "Wien"-er. But the guy who invented the weenie actually studied in Frankfurt. When he moved to Vienna, he named his creation for his old hometown...a Frankfurter. Only in Vienna are *Wieners* called *Frankfurters.* Got it?

Vienna's Café Culture: In Vienna, the living room is down the street at the neighborhood coffeehouse. These classic institutions—many with a tradition stretching back generations—offer newspapers, pastries, sofas, elegant ambience, and "take all the time you want" charm for the price of a cup of coffee. Most serve light lunches, and some might have a more ambitious menu, but the focus here is on drinks. Each classic café has its individual character (and characters). Adopt an unhurried attitude, ignore the sometimes-shabby patina, roll with the famously grumpy waiters, and immerse yourself in the coffee experience, Vienna style.

Vienna—arguably the European birthplace of coffee—serves many of the same drinks (espresso, cappuccino) served in American or Italian coffee shops. There's some uniquely Austrian coffee lingo: A *Mélange* is like a cappuccino, a *Verlängeter* is an Americano, and a *Verkehrt* ("incorrect") is a short latte.

Traditional Austrian Cuisine

Traditional Austrian cooking is meat-heavy and hearty (although fish is very popular and generally good in this landlocked country). Many "Austrian" dishes are actually the legacy of their former empire, which included Hungary and Bohemia.

Main Dishes: The classic Austrian dish—and a stand-by on menus—is Wiener schnitzel (a veal cutlet that's been pounded flat, breaded, and fried). Pork schnitzel, which is cheaper, is also common. Austrian *Gulasch,* a meat stew spiced with onion and paprika, is a favorite comfort food. Chicken and pork come in all varieties—try *Schweinsbraten* (pork with dumplings and sauerkraut). *Tafelspitz* is boiled beef served with vegetables. For a meal-sized salad, order a *Salatteller.*

Sides: Common side dishes include *Knödel* (dumplings), *Spätzle* (little noodles), *Eiernockerl* (egg noodles), potatoes, and salads. *Spargel* (giant asparagus) is a must in early summer. Soups are popular, especially *Speckknödel* (ham-filled dumplings served in broth) and *Frittatensuppe* (beef broth with thin strips of crêpe).

Drinks: Austria specializes in fine boutique wines that are generally not exported and therefore not well-known. The wine (65 percent white) from the Danube River Valley and eastern Austria is particularly good. Good-quality wines are often available by the glass—an *Achtel* (4 oz) or a *Viertel* (8 oz). If you order *"Ein Viertel Weisswein, bitte—trocken,"* you'll get a glass of white wine that's *"trocken"*—dry. *Halbtrocken* is medium, and *süss* is sweet. Austria's signature wine is the *Grüner Veltliner*—a dry white, drunk young, that pairs well with food. In summer, locals also enjoy a refreshing *gespritzer Wein*—wine with sparkling water. Because so many white wines are best young, Austrians enjoy drinking the new wine at wine gardens called *Heurigen* (see page 141).

For beer, Austrians prefer light to dark—lager *(Märzen)* and *Pils.* Also common are *Weissbier* (yeasty and wheat-based), *Bock* (hoppy

Austrian white wines go well with local cuisine.   For beer, try a lager or a lemony *Radler.*

Eating

Eating

Restaurant Price Code

$$$$ **Splurge:** Most main courses over €20
$$$ **Pricier:** €15-20
$$ **Moderate:** €10-15
$ **Budget:** Under €10

Based on the average cost of a typical main course. A wurst stand or other takeout spot is **$**; a beer hall, *Biergarten,* or basic sit-down eatery is **$$**; a casual but more upscale restaurant is **$$$**; and a swanky splurge is **$$$$**.

seasonal ale), and *Radler* (beer with lemon soda). Vienna's local brewery is Ottakringer. When you order beer on tap *(vom Fass),* you can ask for *ein Pfiff* (about 7 oz), *ein Seidel* (10 oz), *ein Krügerl* (17 oz), or *eine Mass* (a whole liter—about a quart).

Austrians enjoy a wide range of local, nonalcoholic spritz drinks such as *Apfelsaft gespritzt* (sparkling apple juice), *Spezi* (Coke and orange soda), and the *über*-Austrian *Almdudler* (ginger ale).

Dessert: While you're sure to have *Apfelstrudel* (apple-pie filling wrapped in wafer-thin pastry), try *Topfenstrudel,* too (with sweet cheese and raisins). *Palatschinken* (sweet filled crêpes) have Hungarian origins. The very Austrian *Kaiserschmarr'n* consists of fluffy, caramelized crêpe strips topped with fruit, raisins, and/or nuts. Everywhere you'll see Mozart Balls *(Mozartkugeln)*—a chocolate confection wrapped with the composer's likeness that's become practically a symbol of Austria. The Fürst brand is handmade and authentic (first made in 1890); other brands are Reber (high quality) and Mirabell (biggest seller). And then there's Vienna's famous chocolate cake—*Sacher torte.* When you order it with "whipped cream," don't use the German word *Schlagsahne*, say *"mit Obers."*

Guten Appetit!

OLD TOWN—NEAR ST. STEPHEN'S CATHEDRAL: All are within a five-minute walk of the cathedral. U: Stephansplatz. (See map page 164.)

①	**$ Gigerl Stadtheuriger** Rauhensteingasse 3 tel. 01/513-4431	Fun *Heuriger* wine cellar experience in city center, traditional buffet, local wine, indoor/outdoor (daily 15:00-24:00)
②	**$$ Zu den Drei Hacken** Singerstrasse 28 tel. 01/512-5895	Fun typical *Weinstube* (wine pub), local specialties, weekday lunch specials, indoor/outdoor (Mon-Sat 11:00-23:00, closed Sun)
③	**$$ Trześniewski** Dorotheergasse 2 tel. 01/512-3291	An institution; build light lunch of finger sandwiches, beer, pay, and get drink token (Mon-Fri 8:30-19:30, Sat 9:00-17:00, closed Sun)
④	**$$$ Cantinetta La Norma** Franziskaner Platz 3 tel. 01/512-8665	Tasty Italian in cozy yet energetic ambience, weekday lunch specials, indoor/outdoor (daily 11:00-24:00)

5	**$$ Reinthaler's Beisl** Dorotheergasse 4 tel. 01/513-1249	Time-warp eatery serving simple, traditional fare; fun, classic interior; outdoor seating (daily 11:00-22:30)
6	**$$ Akakiko Sushi** Singerstrasse 4 mobile 057-333-333	Local chain (several locations), pan-Asian with Japanese emphasis, modern, charmless, fast (daily 10:30-23:30)
7	**$$-$$$ Motto am Fluss Café and Restaurant** Schwedenplatz 2 café tel. 01/252-5511 restaurant tel. 01/252-5510	Views of Danube Canal, classy (cheaper) café with seating inside and out (daily 8:00-24:00); elegant restaurant, lunch specials (daily 11:30-14:30 & 18:00-24:00)

OLD TOWN—NEAR AM HOF SQUARE: This square, just beyond the Graben, is surrounded by atmospheric medieval lanes with charming eateries. U: Herrengasse. (See map page 164.)

8	**$$$ Restaurant Ofenloch** Kurrentgasse 8, tel. 01/533-8844	Traditional Viennese cuisine, formal dressy white-tablecloth service yet relaxed ambience (Mon-Sat 11:00-23:00, closed Sun)
9	**$$ Biobar von Antun** Drahtgasse 3 tel. 01/968-9351	Earthy place on Judenplatz with calm hippie interior and vegan meals (Tue-Sun 11:30-14:30 & 17:30-22:30, closed Mon)
10	**$$$ Hopferl Bierhof** Naglergasse 13 tel. 01/533-4428	Ottakringer beer and meaty food outside on square (daily 11:30-24:00)
11	**$$-$$$ Zum Schwarzen Kameel Wine Bar and Restaurant** Bognergasse 5 tel. 01/533-8125	Office workers grab a stool (in or out), small plates and finger sandwiches, try horseradish and ham (daily 8:00-24:00), elegant pricey restaurant (daily 12:00-24:00)
12	**$$ Café Central** Herrengasse 14 tel. 01/533-3764	Classic historic café, a bit touristy, fancy coffees, breakfasts, weekday lunch specials, main dishes, evening live piano (daily 7:30-22:00, Sun from 10:00)
13	**$ Julius Meinl am Graben** Am Graben 19 tel. 01/532-3334	Famous deli for gourmet takeout picnic fixings, also café and pricey restaurant (Mon-Fri 8:00-19:30, Sat 9:00-18:00, closed Sun)

OLD TOWN—NEAR THE OPERA: These eateries are within easy walking distance of the opera house. U: Karlsplatz, or ride the tram—stop: Oper. (See map page 164.)

⑭	**$$$ Café Restaurant Palmenhaus** Burggarten 1 tel. 01/533-1033	Greenhouse overlooking palm-tree garden, away from crowds, fish specialties (daily 10:00-24:00, shorter winter hours)
⑮	**$ Soho Kantine** Burggarten (just past butterfly house) mobile 0676-309-5161	Cave-like cantina offering unexciting, institutional lunches to locals (Mon-Fri 11:30-15:00, closed Sat-Sun and mid-July-Aug)
⑯	**$$ Kurkonditorei Oberlaa** Neuer Markt 16 tel. 01/5132-9360	Connoisseur quality pastries, light meals, in/out, weekday lunch specials (daily 8:00-20:00)
⑰	**$$ Le Bol Patisserie Bistró** Neuer Markt 14 mobile 0699-1030-1899	Light French food, French-speaking staff, salads, baguette sandwiches, croissants (Mon-Sat 8:00-22:00, Sun 10:00-20:00)
⑱	**$ Billa Corso** Neuer Markt 17 tel. 01/961-2133	Supermarket deli for picnic fixings, also hot meals for takeout or eat in (Mon-Fri 8:00-20:00, Sat until 19:00)

MUSEUM DISTRICT—SPITTELBERG: Charming cobbled grid of traffic-free lanes and tables tumbling down sidewalks and into breezy courtyards; handy for Mariahilfer Strasse hotels; browse Spittelberggasse, Gutenberggasse, and Schrankgasse; great in summer, dead in bad weather. U: Volkstheater/Museumsplatz. (See map page 166.)

⑲	**$ Amerlingbeisl** Stiftgasse 8 tel. 01/526 1660	Charming, casual vine-covered courtyard on cobbled street; Austrian, international, some vegetarian (daily 9:00-24:00)
⑳	**$$$ Zu Ebener Erde und Erster Stock** Burggasse 13 tel. 01/523-6254 www.zu-ebener-erde-und-erster-stock.at	Traditional fare, choose casual woody downstairs or fancy red-velvet upstairs, or outside, reservations smart (Mon-Fri 12:00-22:00, closed Sat-Sun)
㉑	**$$ Glacis Beisl** Breitegasse 4 tel. 01/526-5660	Breezy wine garden for locals, weekday lunch specials (daily 11:00-24:00)

Eating

Eating

㉒ **$$ Plutzer Bräu** Schrankgasse 4 tel. 01/526-1215	Sprawling brewpub serving stick-to-your-ribs pub grub, Tirolean beers, and home brews (daily 11:00-24:00)
㉓ **$-$$ City Hall** **Food Circus** Rathausplatz	City Hall park hosts lively outdoor food fair nightly July-Aug (see page 189).

MARIAHILFER STRASSE AND THE NASCHMARKT: The street is lined with reasonable cafés serving all types of cuisine. A short walk away are Spittelberg (see earlier) and the Naschmarkt. U: Neubaugasse or Zieglergasse. (See map page 166.)

㉔ **$$ Trześniewski** Mariahilfer Strasse 95 tel. 01/596-4291)	Same sandwiches as ➌ but minus the ambience (Mon-Fri 8:30-19:00, Sat 9:00-18:00, closed Sun)
㉕ **$ Schnitzelwirt** Neubaugasse 52 tel. 01/523-3771	Huge, cheap schnitzels and *gulasch* in smoky working-class 1950s place (Mon-Sat 11:00-21:30, closed Sun)
㉖ **Merkur** Mariahilfer Strasse 42	Supermarket for picnic fixings (Mon-Fri until 20:00, Sat until 18:00, closed Sun)
㉗ **$$ Café Sperl** Gumpendorfer 11 tel. 01/586-4158	Classic 1880 café still furnished identically to the day it opened (Mon-Sat 7:00-23:00, Sun 11:00-20:00, closed Sun July-Aug)
㉘ **$-$$ Naschmarkt** Wienzeile street	Multiblock open-air market (see page 132) with produce stalls, cafés, ethnic food, wursts, also fashionable for dinner (Mon-Fri 6:00-18:30, Sat until 17:00, closed Sun, closes earlier in winter)

Restaurants in Central Vienna

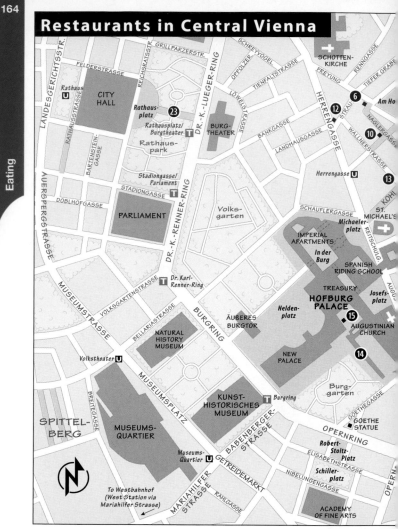

SCHOTTEN-KIRCHE

RENNGASSE

TIEFER GRABE

FELDERSTRASSE

GRILLPARZERSTR

REICHSRATSSTR.

SCHREYVOGEL

OPPOLZER

TIENFALTSTRASSE

FREYUNG

LANDESGERICHTSSTR.

RATHAUSSTRASSE

Rathaus U

CITY HALL

Rathaus-platz **23**

Rathausplatz/Burgtheater T

Rathaus-park

DR. - K. - LUEGER-RING

LÖWELSTRASSE

BURG-THEATER

HERRENGASSE

STRAU

WALLNERSTRASSE

NAGLERGASSE

6

Am Ho

12

10

BARTENSTEIN-GASSE

DOBLHOFGASSE

STADIONGASSE

Stadiongasse/Parlament T

BANKGASSE

LANDHAUSGASSE

Herrengasse U

13

AUERSPERGSTRASSE

DR. - K. - RENNER-RING

PARLIAMENT

Volks-garten

SCHAUFLERGASSE

KOHL

ST. MICHAEL'S

MUSEUMSTRASSE

VOLKSGARTENSTRASSE

Dr. Karl-Renner-Ring T

Michaeler-platz

IMPERIAL APARTMENTS

In der Burg

REITSCHUL

SPANISH RIDING SCHOOL

BELLARIASTRASSE

BURGRING

ÄUSSERES BURGTOR

Helden-platz

TREASURY

HOFBURG PALACE

15

Josefs-platz

AUGU

NATURAL HISTORY MUSEUM

Volkstheater U

AUGUSTINIAN CHURCH

NEW PALACE

14

BREITEGASSE

SPITTEL-BERG

MUSEUMSPLATZ

KUNST-HISTORISCHES MUSEUM

Burgring T

Burg-garten

GOETHEGASSE

GOETHE STATUE

OPERNRING

BABENBERGER-STRASSE

Robert-Stoltz-Platz

ELISABETHSTRASSE

MUSEUMS-QUARTIER

Museums-Quartier U

GETREIDEMARKT

MARIAHILFER STRASSE

RAHLGASSE

NIBELUNGENGASSE

Schiller-platz

OPERN

To Westbahnhof (West Station via Mariahilfer Strasse)

ACADEMY OF FINE ARTS

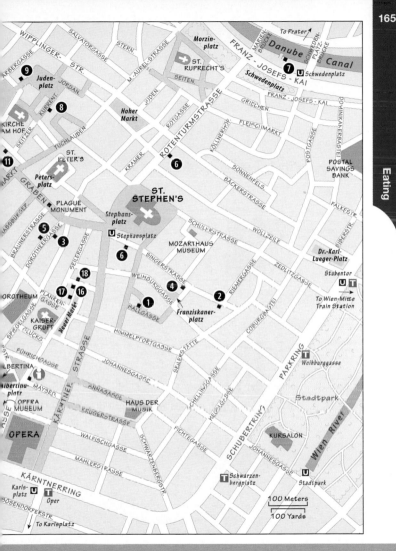

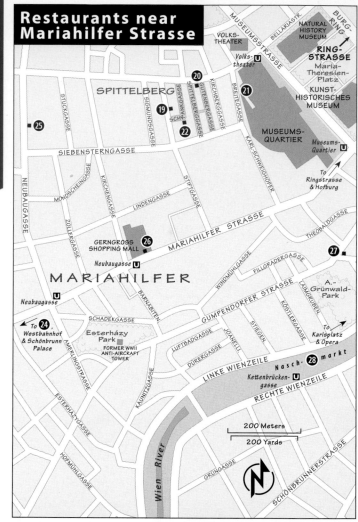

Restaurants near Mariahilfer Strasse

BURG-RING

NATURAL HISTORY MUSEUM

RING-STRASSE

Maria-Theresien-Platz

KUNST-HISTORISCHES MUSEUM

MUSEUMSSTRASSE

BELLARIASTR.

VOLKS-THEATER

Volks-theater U

BREITEGASSE

KIRCHBERGGASSE

SPITTELBERGGASSE

GUTENBERGGASSE

SIGMUNDSGASSE

STUCKGASSE

SPITTELBERG

20

19

SCH...

22

25

SIEBENSTERNGASSE

NEUBAUGASSE

ZOLLERGASSE

MONDSCHEINGASSE

KIRCHENGASSE

LINDENGASSE

STIFTGASSE

KARL-SCHWEIGHOFER-

MUSEUMS-QUARTIER

Museums-Quartier U

To Ringstrasse & Hofburg

THEOBALDGASSE

MARIAHILFER STRASSE

GERNGROSS SHOPPING MALL

26

Neubaugasse U

MARIAHILFER

Neubaugasse U

BARNABITEN

WINDMÜHLGASSE

FILLGRADERGASSE

27

A.-Grünwald-Park

To Karlsplatz & Opera

GUMPENDORFER STRASSE

KÖSTLERGASSE

LÄMGRUBEN

To Westbahnhof & Schönbrunn Palace

24

SCHADEKGASSE

Esterházy Park

FORMER WWII ANTI-AIRCRAFT TOWER

AMERLINGSTRASSE

KAUNITZGASSE

LUFTBADGASSE

DÜRERGASSE

JOANELLI

STIEGEN

LINKE WIENZEILE

Nasch- markt

28

Kettenbrücken-gasse U

RECHTE WIENZEILE

ESTERHÁZYGASSE

HOFMÜHLGASSE

GRÜNGASSE

SCHÖNBRUNNERSTRASSE

Wien River

200 Meters

200 Yards

N

Practicalities

PLANNING

When to Go

Vienna's best travel months—also the busiest and most expensive for flights and hotels—are roughly May through September. Summer brings the best weather (it's rarely too hot), long sightseeing days, and big tourist crowds. "Shoulder season" (spring and fall) is a bit less expensive and less crowded, with decent weather and more flexible hotel prices. Vienna in winter is cold and rainy, but its cafés are cozy, Christmas markets bustle, the concert seasons are in full swing, and Vienna hosts its famous balls.

Know Before You Go

Make sure your passport is up to date (to renew, see www.travel.state. gov). Tell your debit- and credit-card companies about your plans. Book hotel rooms well in advance if you'll be traveling during peak season or any major holidays or festivals. Consider buying travel insurance (see www. ricksteves.com/insurance). Vienna's museums don't require long-range planning for advance tickets, but consider reserving ahead for Schönbrunn Palace (summer and weekends, see page 112) for the Lipizzaner stallions (see page 123), and for major musical events such as the Vienna State Opera (see page 185) and the Vienna Boys' Choir (see page 188). If you're traveling beyond Vienna, this centrally located city is an excellent jumping-off point by train to neighboring countries. There are good bargains for rail passes and discount tickets: Do your research.

MONEY

Austria uses the euro currency: 1 euro (€1) = about $1.10. To convert euros to dollars add about 10 percent: €20 = about $22, €50 = about $55. (Check www.oanda.com for the latest exchange rates.)

Withdraw money from an ATM (known as a *Bankomat* in Austria) using a debit card, just like at home. Visa and MasterCard are commonly used throughout Europe. Before departing, call your bank or credit-card company: Confirm that your card will work overseas, ask about international transaction fees, alert them that you'll be making withdrawals in

Helpful Websites

Vienna Tourist Information: www.vienna.info
Austrian Tourist Information: www.austria.info
Passports and Red Tape: www.travel.state.gov
Cheap Flights: www.kayak.com
Airplane Carry-on Restrictions: www.tsa.gov
European Train Schedules: www.bahn.com
General Travel Tips: www.ricksteves.com (train travel, rail passes, car rental, staying connected, travel insurance, packing lists, and much more—plus updates to this book)

Europe, and if you don't know it, get your credit card PIN. Many travelers bring a second debit/credit card as a backup. Cash is always good to have on hand, so withdraw large amounts (€250-300) from the ATM.

While American credit cards are accepted almost everywhere in Europe, even newer chip-style cards may not work in some payment machines (e.g., ticket kiosks). If your card is rejected, be prepared to pay with cash, find a nearby cashier who can swipe it, or try entering your PIN.

To keep your cash and valuables safe, wear a money belt. If you lose your credit or debit card, report the loss immediately with a collect phone call: Visa (tel. 303/967-1096), MasterCard (tel. 636/722-7111), and American Express (tel. 336/393-1111).

Get money from ATMs, just like at home.

Credit cards are OK, but keep cash on hand.

Practicalities

ARRIVAL IN VIENNA

Vienna International Airport

The airport has plenty of services in the arrivals hall—TI, shops, ATMs, eateries, and a supermarket (airport code: VIE, airport tel. 01/700-722-233, www.viennaairport.com).

To get between the airport and downtown Vienna (12 miles away), you have several options:

Bus: Convenient express airport buses go to various points in Vienna: Morzinplatz/Schwedenplatz U-Bahn station (for city-center hotels, 20 minutes), Westbahnhof (for Mariahilfer Strasse hotels, 45 minutes), and Wien-Meidling Bahnhof (30 minutes). Buy your ticket from the driver and double check your destination with him (€8, 2/hour, tel. 0810-222-333, www.viennaairportlines.at).

Suburban Train (S-Bahn): The S-7 connects with Wien-Mitte Bahnhof, on the east side of the Ring (described later), where you can transfer to the subway (U-Bahn) or taxi to the city center and recommended hotels. From the arrivals hall, go down the ramps, following red ÖBB signs, to the train station. Buy a regular two-zone public transport ticket (€4.40, includes transfers) from the multilingual red "Fahrkarten" machines. Trains to downtown (24 minutes, 2/hour) are marked *Floridsdorf.* Another option is the express CAT train, which costs €12 and takes 16 minutes. Follow the green signage and buy a ticket from the green machines (www.cityairporttrain.com).

Taxi: The 30-minute ride into town costs a fixed €36 from the several companies with desks in the arrivals hall. If you take a taxi from the taxi rank outside, you'll pay the metered rate, which should come out about the same.

Vienna's Train Stations

Vienna has several train stations, so be sure to confirm which station your train uses. All stations have a *Reisezentrum* (Travel Center) where you can ask questions and buy tickets, and all have easy public transit options to the city center.

Wien Hauptbahnhof, the main station, is south of downtown. To reach the city center, ride the U-1 (direction: Leopoldau) to Karlsplatz, Stephansplatz, or Schwedenplatz, or take tram #D (which runs along the Ring). To reach Mariahilfer Strasse, hop on bus #13A. **Westbahnhof,** west

The renovated Hauptbahnhof (main train station) is an easy U-Bahn, tram, or bus ride from the center.

of downtown, has many user-friendly shops and services. To reach the city center, follow orange signs to the U-3 (direction: Simmering). If your hotel is along Mariahilfer Strasse, either take the U-3 or just walk. **Franz-Josefs-Bahnhof,** to the north, connects to the center by the convenient tram #D. **Wien-Mitte Bahnhof** is where airport trains arrive and depart. To get to the city center, take the U-3 (from the station's U-Bahn stop, called "Landstrasse") to hotels near Stephansplatz or Mariahilfer Strasse, or the U-4 to hotels closer to the airport.

Tips for Drivers

Approaching Vienna on the A-1 expressway from Melk or Salzburg, pass Schönbrunn Palace and turn left onto the Gürtel to reach Mariahilfer Strasse hotels, or continue on to reach the city center. Approaching from Krems on A-22, cross the Danube at the fourth bridge (Reichsbrücke). At the big roundabout, take the second right onto Praterstrasse. Once on the Ringstrasse, circle around until you reach the "spoke" street you need. Don't use your car to sightsee in traffic-unfriendly Vienna. Ask if your hotel provides discounted parking, or leave it at a garage.

HELPFUL HINTS

Tourist Information (TI): Vienna's main TI is behind the Vienna State Opera at Albertinaplatz (daily 9:00-19:00, Wi-Fi, theater box office, tel. 01/211-140, www.vienna.info). There are also TIs at the airport (daily 7:00-22:00) and train station (daily 9:00-19:00). Look for the monthly program of concerts, called *Wien-Programm*. Ask about the program of guided walks, and consider buying a Vienna Pass (described later).

Hurdling the Language Barrier: Most Viennese, especially those in the tourist trade, speak at least some English. Still, you'll get more smiles by using a few German pleasantries. It's polite to greet your fellow travelers in the hotel breakfast room in the morning *("Gute Morgen")* and greet shop owners as you enter *("Grüss Gott"*—"Hi"). The Austrian form of German isn't much different from the *Deutsch* spoken by Germans—but those small differences are a big deal to Austrians. For example, the German *Guten Tag* sounds oddly uptight to Austrians, who prefer *Grüss Gott*—literally "May God greet you." Tacking an *-l* or *-erl* on the end of a word makes it a diminutive form—like adding "-ette" or "-ie" to an English word. Austrians appreciate any effort on your part to speak their language, even if it's just a little bit—*ein Bissl*. To learn a few more German phrases, see page 193.

Time Zones: Austria's time zone is six/nine hours ahead of the east/west coasts of the US.

Business Hours: Most shops are open Monday through Saturday from about 9:00 until 18:00-20:00, but close earlier on Saturday and are almost always closed on Sunday. Most banks are open weekdays roughly from 8:00 until 15:00.

Watt's Up? Europe's electrical system is 220 volts, instead of North America's 110 volts. You'll need an adapter plug with two round prongs, sold inexpensively at travel stores in the US. Most newer electronics (such as phones, laptops, hair dryers, and battery chargers) convert automatically, so you won't need a separate converter.

Numbers and Stumblers: What Americans call the second floor of a building is the first floor in Europe. Europeans write dates as day/month/year. Commas are decimal points and vice versa—a dollar and half is 1,50, and there are 5.280 feet in a mile. Austria uses the metric system: A kilogram is 2.2 pounds; a liter is about a quart; and a kilometer is six-tenths of a mile. Temperature is measured in Celsius: 0°C = 32°F. To roughly convert Celsius to Fahrenheit, double the number and add 30.

Don't Go Bezirk: Addresses start with the *Bezirk* (district) number,

Tipping

Tipping in Austria isn't as generous as it is in the US. To tip a taxi driver, round up your fare a bit (for a €4.50 fare, give €5). For longer rides, figure about 5-10 percent. At hotels, if you let the porter carry your luggage, tip a euro for each bag. For sit-down service in a restaurant, a service charge is generally already included in the bill. However, if you feel the service was exceptional, it's fine to tip 5-10 percent extra.

followed by the street and building number. The first district is the Old Town (inside the Ring). Any address higher than the ninth *Bezirk* is beyond the Gürtel, far from the center. So the address "7, Lindengasse 4" is in the seventh district, #4 on Linden Lane.

Wi-Fi: You'll find free hotspots around town, including at the TI, Hauptbahnhof, Westbahnhof, Stephansplatz, Naschmarkt, City Hall Park, Prater Park, and Donauinsel.

English Bookstore: Stop by the woody and cool Shakespeare & Co., in an atmospheric district near the Danube Canal (Mon-Fri 9:00-21:00, Sat 9:00-20:00, closed Sun, north of Hoher Markt at Sterngasse 2, tel. 01/535-5053, www.shakespeare.co.at). If you want English newspapers, read them for free with class in Vienna's marvelous coffeehouses.

Post Office: The main post office is near Schwedenplatz at Fleischmarkt 19 (open daily). Convenient branch offices are at the Hauptbahnhof, Westbahnhof, and near the opera house (Krugerstrasse 13).

Laundry: Schnell & Sauber Waschcenter is close to Mariahilfer Strasse accommodations, and easily reached from downtown by U-Bahn (free Wi-Fi; daily 6:00-24:00, Westbahnstrasse 60, U: Burggasse/Stadthalle, mobile 0660-760-4546, www.schnellundsauber.at).

Travel Agency: Conveniently located on Stephansplatz, Ruefa sells tickets for flights, trains, and boats to Bratislava (Mon-Fri 9:00-18:30, closed Sat-Sun, Stephansplatz 10, tel. 01/513-4000, Gertrude and Sandra speak English).

Drinking Water: The Viennese are proud of their perfectly drinkable tap water from alpine springs. You'll spot locals refilling their little bottles at fountains all over town.

GETTING AROUND VIENNA

Vienna's historic core inside the Ring is walkable, but you'll want to use public transit to get elsewhere.

By Tram, Bus, and Metro

Take full advantage of Vienna's efficient transit system, which includes trams, buses, and a metro system of U-Bahn (subway) and S-Bahn (faster suburban) trains. The TI's free Vienna city map includes a small transit map. Transit info: Tel. 01/790-9100, www.wienerlinien.at.

Tickets: A single ticket costs €2.20 (€2.30 on tram or bus) and is good for one journey with necessary transfers on the tram, bus, U-Bahn, or S-Bahn. Transit passes come in 24-hour (€7.60), 48-hour (€13.30), and 72-hour (€16.50) options. A seven-day pass (*Wochenkarte,* €16.20) runs from Monday to Monday. The eight-day "Climate Ticket" (*Acht-Tage-Klimakarte,* €38.40) can be shared, making it a real saver for groups.

Buy tickets from vending machines in stations (marked *Fahrkarten/Ticket,* easy and in English), from *Vorverkauf* offices in stations, or on trams or buses (single tickets only).

Riding Transit: To get your bearings on trams, buses, the U-Bahn, and the S-Bahn, you'll want to know the end-of-the-line stop in the direction that you're heading. For example, to ride from Stephansplatz to the Hauptbahnhof on the U-1, you'd be going in the direction "Reumannplatz." You must stamp your ticket at the barriers in U-Bahn and S-Bahn stations, and in the machines on trams and buses (stamp multiple-use passes only the first time you board). Cheaters pay a stiff €100 fine.

On trams, stop announcements are voice-only and easy to miss—carry a map. Rookies miss stops because they fail to open the door. Push

Rent a bike at stations like this.

Use trams to expand your sightseeing.

buttons, pull latches—do whatever it takes. Before you exit a U-Bahn station, study the wall-mounted street map. Choosing the right exit saves lots of walking.

Helpful Lines: The map on page 176 shows some of the most helpful lines for readers of this book. I generally stick to the tram to zip around the Ring (trams #1, #2, #D, and #O) and take the U-Bahn to outlying sights, hotels, and Vienna's train stations. Cute little electric bus #1A is great for a joyride through the historic center: Hop on and see where it takes you.

By Taxi, Uber, or Private Driver

Vienna's comfortable, civilized, and easy-to-flag-down **taxis** start at €3.80. You'll pay about €10 to go from the opera house to the Hauptbahnhof. Pay only what's on the meter—the only legitimate surcharges are for calling a cab (€3), riding to the airport (€13), and a night charge.

If you like **Uber,** the ride service (and your app) works in Vienna just like it does in the US.

Johann (a.k.a. John) Lichtl is a gentle, honest, English-speaking cabbie who runs his own **private taxi service** within Vienna and does driving tours to nearby destinations (mobile 0676-670-6750, €27/1 hour, €27 to or from airport, day trip to the Danube Valley-€160, Mauthausen-€240).

By Bike

With more than 600 miles of bike lanes (and a powerful Green Party), Vienna is a great city on two wheels. The bike path along the Ring (following my Ringstrasse Tram Tour on page 52) is wonderfully entertaining. Or trace a route from Stadtpark (City Park), across Danube Island, and out to the modern Donau City business district. These routes are easy to follow using the free city map available at the TI (some routes can be downloaded from TI website).

Citybike Wien lets you rent (sturdy if heavy) bikes from over 100 public racks scattered through the city center. To borrow one, register your credit card at the terminal at any rack, create a password (save it for future rentals), then unlock a bike (you can also register online). First-time registration is €1 (only one bike per credit card, first hour-free, second hour-€1, third hour-€2, €4/hour after that, toll tel. 0810-500-500, www.citybikewien.at).

Pedal Power, near Prater Park, rents better-quality bikes, offers bike tours (from location near opera house), and provides good biking info (€6/hour, 4 hours-€19, 24 hours-€30, ask about Rick Steves discount, daily

Practicalities

Vienna's Public Transportation

To Franz-Josefs-Bahnhof & Nussdorf

Schlick-gasse

#D

Schottentor

#1

Schottentor

#38

To Nussdorferstrasse & Grinzing

To Nussdorferstrasse & Floridsdorf

Ottakring

U-6

Alser Str. / Skodagasse

Rathaus

RAT-HAUS

#D

RINGSTRASSE TRAM TOUR

#13 A

#1 #D

Rathaus / Burgtheater

U-3

#2

Ledergasse

U-2

Stadiongasse Parlament

OLD

IMPERIAL FURNITURE COLLECTION

Zieglergasse

Neubaugasse

#1 #2 #D

Herrengasse

WEST-BAHNHOF

Dr.-Karl-Renner-Ring

U-3

MARIAHILFER STRASSE

Volkstheater

U-2

HOFBURG

KUNST-HIST. MUSEUM

Burgring

#1 #2 #D

Museums-quartier

U-6

#58

#13 A

To Hüttel-dorf U-4

Hietzing

Schönbrunn

Längenfeld-gasse

U-4

Pilgramgasse

SCHÖNBRUNN PALACE

#62

#1

BAHNHOF MEIDLING

To Siebenhirten

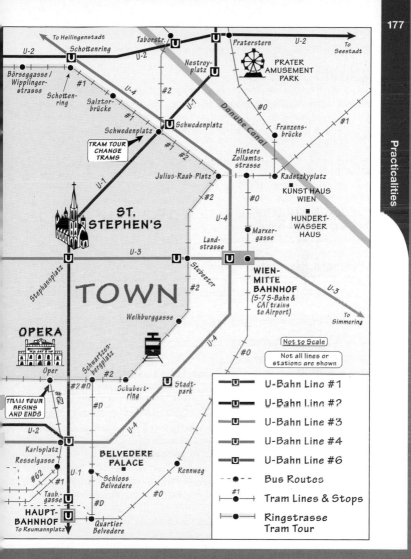

To Heilingenstadt

Schottenring

U-2

Taborstr.

Praterstern

U-2

To Seestadt

Nestroy-platz

U-2

PRATER AMUSEMENT PARK

Börseggasse / Wipplinger-strasse

#1

Schotten-ring

U-4

Danube Canal

#0

Franzens-brücke

#1

Salztor-brücke

Schwedenplatz

#1

TRAM TOUR CHANGE TRAMS

#1

#2

Hintere Zollamts-strasse

Radetzkyplatz

Julius-Raab Platz

#2

#0

KUNST HAUS WIEN

U-1

#2

U-4

HUNDERT-WASSER HAUS

ST. STEPHEN'S

Marxer-gasse

U-3

Stephansplatz

Land-strasse

WIEN-MITTE BAHNHOF

TOWN

Stubentor

(S-7 S-Bahn & CAT trains to Airport)

U-3

Weihburggasse

#2

To Simmering

U-4

OPERA

Not to Scale

Not all lines or stations are shown

Oper

Schwarzen-bergplatz

#2 #D

#0

TRAM TOUR BEGINS AND ENDS

Schubert-ring

U-2

Stadt-park

U-4

Karlsplatz

Resselgasse

U-1

BELVEDERE PALACE

Rennweg

#62

#1

Schloss Belvedere

#0

Taub-gasse

#D

HAUPT-BAHNHOF

Quartier Belvedere

To Reumannplatz

	U-Bahn Line #1
	U-Bahn Line #2
	U-Bahn Line #3
	U-Bahn Line #4
	U-Bahn Line #6
- • -	Bus Routes
⊢•⊣ #1	Tram Lines & Stops
⊢•⊣	Ringstrasse Tram Tour

May-Sept 8:30-18:00, shorter hours May and Oct, Ausstellungsstrasse 3, tel. 01/729-7234, www.pedalpower.at).

STAYING CONNECTED

You can bring your own mobile device (phone, tablet, laptop) and follow my budget tips. Or buy a European SIM card for your phone. You can also use European landlines (in your hotel room) and computers (there's usually one in your hotel lobby). These options are described in full at www.ricksteves.com/phoning.

Making Calls

To **call Austria from a US or Canadian phone:** Dial 011 (international access code), 43 (Austria's country code), and the phone number.

To **call Austria from a European phone:** Dial 00, then 43 followed by the phone number.

To **make calls within Austria,** just dial the phone number, including the initial 0 if present.

To **call from Austria to another country:** Dial 00, the country code (for example, 1 for the US or Canada), then the number.

Initial Zero: Drop the initial zero from international phone numbers (except when calling Italy).

Mobile Tip: Pressing the + sign auto-selects the correct international access code.

Budget Tips for Using Your Mobile Device in Europe

Use free Wi-Fi whenever possible. Unless you have an unlimited data plan, save most of your online tasks for Wi-Fi. Many hotels and cafés have Wi-Fi for guests.

Sign up for an international plan. Most providers offer a global plan that cuts the cost of calls and texts, and gives you a block of data. Your normal plan may already include international coverage.

Minimize the use of your cellular network. If you can't find Wi-Fi, you can roam on your cellular network. When you're done, avoid further charges by disabling cellular data or roaming in your settings. Save bandwidth-gobbling tasks (Skyping, downloading apps, streaming) for when you're on Wi-Fi.

Use calling/messaging apps for cheaper calls and texts. Some

Useful Phone Numbers

Police, Fire, and Ambulance: Tel. 112

US Embassy in Vienna: Boltzmanngasse 16, tel. 01/313-390, ViennaUSEmbassy@state.gov; consular services at Parkring 12, daily 8:00-11:30, tel. 01/313-397-535, http://Austria.usembassy.gov, consulatevienna@state.gov

Canadian Embassy in Vienna: Laurenzerberg 2, 3rd floor, Mon-Fri 8:00-12:30, tel. 01/531-383-000, after-hours emergencies call collect Canadian tel. 613/996-8885, www.austria.gc.ca, vienn@international.gc.ca

apps (Skype, Viber, FaceTime, Google+ Hangouts) let you call or text for free or cheap when you're on Wi-Fi.

Buy a European SIM card: This option helps you get faster data connections and make voice calls at cheap local rates. Buy a basic phone in Europe (about $40 from a phone shop) or bring an "unlocked" US phone from home. Once you insert a European SIM, you'll have a European phone number. Buy a new card when you arrive in a new country (sold at phone shops, newsstands, vending machines, and department-store electronics counters).

Stick to landlines: If it's inexpensive to make calls from your hotel-room phone (ask at the desk for rates before you dial), you can make your calls even cheaper by using an international phone card (sold at many newsstands, street kiosks, tobacco shops, and train stations).

SIGHTSEEING TIPS

Hours: Hours of sights can change unexpectedly, so confirm the latest times at the TI, at the sight's website, or at the general website www.vienna.info. Many sights stop admitting people 30-60 minutes before closing time, and guards start ushering people out before the actual closing time, so don't save the best for last.

What to Expect: Many sights (such as Schönbrunn) have metal detectors or conduct bag searches that will slow your entry. Some require you to check even small daypacks and coats—usually for free.

Photos and videos are normally allowed, but flashes or tripods usually are not. Many sights offer guided tours and rent audioguides (€3-6). Expect changes—artwork can be in restoration or on tour. Most sights have an on-site café.

Discounts: Seniors (age 60 and over), youths under 19, and students or teachers with proper identification cards (www.isic.org) can get discounts at many sights. Always ask. Some discounts are available only for citizens of the European Union.

🎧 **Free Rick Steves Audio Tours:** I've produced free audio tours of several of Vienna's best sights, including the Vienna City Walk, St. Stephen's Cathedral Tour, and my Ringstrasse Tram Tour. You can download Rick Steves Audio Europe via Apple's App Store, Google Play, or the Amazon Appstore.

Sightseeing Combo-Tickets

While you can easily buy **advance tickets online** for some sights (from their websites), Vienna's ticket lines aren't as bad as in other cities, so it's not really necessary—especially if you follow my other crowd-avoiding tips, such as arriving early or visiting late. The one place where an advance ticket is really recommended is Schönbrunn Palace in summer and on good-weather weekends (get details on page 112).

More helpful are **combo-tickets** that cover several venues at a single price. If you're seeing those sights anyway, a combo-ticket can save you money and let you skip ticket-buying lines at your next sight. Buy the following combo-tickets at any of the participating sights:

Sisi Ticket: This €29 ticket covers the Hofburg Imperial Apartments (see page 65) as well as Schönbrunn Palace's Grand Tour and the Imperial Furniture Collection. At Schönbrunn, the ticket lets you enter the palace immediately, without a reserved entry time.

Hofburg Treasury and Kunsthistorisches Museum/New Palace: If you're seeing the Hofburg Treasury (royal regalia and crown jewels) and the Kunsthistorisches Museum (world-class art collection), this €20 combo-ticket is well worth it (and you get the New Palace as a bonus).

Haus der Musik and Mozarthaus: The Haus der Musik (mod museum with interactive exhibits) has a combo deal with Mozarthaus Vienna (exhibits and artifacts about the great composer) for €18—saving a few euros for music lovers.

The much-promoted €25 **Vienna Card** (www.wienkarte.at) is not

Austria Almanac

Official Name: Republik Österreich ("Eastern Realm"), or simply Österreich.

Population: Of Austria's 8.6 million people, 91 percent are ethnic Austrians. Three out of four are Catholic; about one in 20 is Muslim.

Geography: Austria is similar in size to South Carolina, and sits at the same latitude as Minnesota. The northeast is flat and well-populated; the southwest has the less-populated Alps. The Danube River meanders 1,770 miles west-to-east, passing through Vienna.

Biggest Cities: One in five Austrians lives in the capital of Vienna (1.8 million in city center). Graz has 275,000 people; Linz has 200,000.

Economy: Austria borders eight other European countries and is well-integrated into the EU economy. Its per-capita Gross Domestic Product of $47,500 is among Europe's highest. One of its biggest moneymakers is tourism, but also wood, paper products...and Red Bull Energy Drink.

Government: The government is headed by a chancellor, with a bicameral legislature. Austria has been officially neutral since 1955, and its citizens take a dim view of European unity. Austria is the only EU nation with a minimum voting age of 16.

Flag: Three horizontal bands of red, white, and red.

The Average Austrian: A typical Austrian is 43 years old, has 1.4 children, and will live to be 81. He or she inhabits a 900-square-foot home, and spends leisure time with a circle of a few close friends. Chances are high that someone in that circle is a smoker—Austrians are among the highest consumers of cigarettes in Europe.

Mellow: Unlike Germany, its industrious neighbor to the northwest, Austria is content to bask in its good living and opulent past as the former head of one of Europe's grandest empires. Austrians are relaxed, gregarious people who love the outdoors as much as a good cup of coffee in a café. *Gemütlichkeit* is the word most often used to describe this special Austrian cozy-and-easy approach to life.

worth the mental overhead for most travelers. It gives you a 72-hour transit pass and minor discounts at the city's museums.

THEFT AND EMERGENCIES

Theft: While violent crime is rare in the city center, thieves (mainly pickpockets) thrive near famous monuments, on public transportation, at places of drunkenness, in hostels, or anywhere crowds press together. Be alert to the possibility of theft, especially when you're absorbed in the wonder and newness of Vienna. I keep my valuables—passport, credit cards, crucial documents, and large amounts of cash—in a money belt that I tuck under my clothes. Dial 112 for English-speaking police help. To replace a passport, file the police report, then call your embassy to make an appointment.

Medical Help: Dial 112 for a medical emergency. Most doctors speak English. For minor ailments, do as the Austrians do and first visit a pharmacy, where qualified technicians routinely diagnose and prescribe. To find a pharmacy or doctor, ask your hotelier for assistance.

Use a money belt for large amounts of cash, credit cards, and passport. It tucks under your clothes.

ACTIVITIES

Shopping

Vienna—a city that loves beautiful things—brings out the shopper in almost everyone. You won't need a guidebook to find plenty of shops selling Sisi fridge magnets, Klimt jewel-cases, Beethoven music boxes, and the ubiquitous Mozart Balls.

If you're more interested in browsing and window shopping, here are a few good neighborhoods: The narrow streets north and west of the cathedral are sprinkled with old fashioned shops that seem to belong to another era—old clocks, men's ties, gloves, and so on. Dedicated window shoppers will enjoy the Dorotheum auction house (see page 128). Mariahilfer Strasse (near recommended hotels) has the major department stores. The Naschmarkt lets you browse edible goodies in a people-watching environment (see page 132).

Vienna's museum shops are some of Europe's best for art-related curios. Try the Albertina Museum, Kunsthistorisches Museum, Belvedere Palace, and the MuseumsQuartier museums. If you're looking for a shop selling traditional dress-up Austrian folk clothing (dirndls and felt suits), the most central is Loden-Plankl (across from the Hofburg, at Michaelerplatz 6); the most authentic is Tostmann Trachten (near Am Hof, at Schottengasse 3A). For the best in Austrian design and handicrafts, visit Österreichische Werkstätten, a shop/gallery just south of the cathedral (Kärntner Strasse 6).

Getting a VAT Refund: If you purchase more than €75.01 worth of goods at a single store, you may be eligible to get a refund of the 20 percent Value-Added Tax (VAT). Have the store fill out the paperwork, then get

Folk clothing is dressy (and pricey).

The Naschmarkt has food and shops.

it stamped at the airport (or border crossing) by customs and processed by a VAT refund company (e.g., Global Blue or Premier Tax/Travelex, located in the airport departure area). Get more details from your merchant or see www.ricksteves.com/vat.

Customs for American Shoppers: You are allowed to take home $800 worth of items per person duty-free, once every 31 days. You can also bring in one liter of alcohol. As for food, you can take home many processed and packaged foods (e.g., vacuum-packed cheeses, chocolate, mustard) but no fresh produce or meats. Any liquid-containing foods must be packed in checked luggage, a potential recipe for disaster. To check customs rules and duty rates, visit www.cbp.gov.

Entertainment and Nightlife

Take in a concert, opera, or other musical event. Enjoy a leisurely dinner (and people-watching) in the stately old town or the atmospheric Spittelberg quarter. Or spend an evening enjoying art, watching a classic film, or sipping Viennese wine in a village wine garden. Save some energy for Vienna after dark.

For a list of current events, pick up the TI's free booklet, *Wien-Programm.* This essential entertainment guide lists music, theater, walks, and museum exhibits, including schedules for the Spanish Riding School, Vienna Boys' Choir, and Vienna State Opera. For a list of events online, try www.wien.info.

Classical Music

Vienna—the birthplace of what we call classical music—still thrives as Europe's music capital. On any given evening, you'll have your choice of opera, Strauss waltzes, Mozart chamber concerts, and lighthearted musicals.

In Vienna, it's music *con brio* from September through June, reaching a symphonic climax during the Vienna Festival each May and June. In July and August, the serious music companies are—like you—on vacation. But even then, music lovers have options.

To sort through Vienna's many musical events, the best overall resource is the ticket box office in the TI on Albertinaplatz. You can also get a good schedule in the monthly *Wien-Programm* or at www.viennaconcerts.com.

The major orchestral venues are the Wiener Musikverein (home to the Vienna Philharmonic Orchestra), and the Wiener Konzerthaus (various events). Most concert tickets run €45-60 (though some venues start around €30). You'll also pay a stiff booking fee reserving by phone, online, or through a box office like the one at the TI. There's no ticket fee if you buy directly at the venue an hour or two before performance time. Call the hall and ask if they expect tickets to be available. There are often people selling their extra tickets at face value or less outside the door before concert time. Many venues offer cheap standing-room tickets (generally an hour before each performance).

Vienna State Opera (Wiener Staatsoper)

This glorious venue along the Ringstrasse belts out world-class opera 300 days a year (Sept-June). As it's subsidized by the state, the company works hard to make opera affordable and accessible to connoisseurs and tourists alike. Dress is casual (but do your best). Main-floor seats go for €120-200; bargain hunters get limited-view seats for €13-30. You can book in advance (tel. 01/513-1513, daily 10:00-21:00, or at www.wiener-staatsoper.at). In person, there are box offices on both the east and west sides of the building (open Mon-Fri 9:00 until two hours before performance, Sat 9:00-12:00, closed Sun).

Unless Placido Domingo is in town, it's easy to get one of 567 **standing-room tickets** (€3-4). Tickets go on sale 80 minutes before show time. Enter on the west side of the opera house (middle of the building). Walk straight in, then head right until you see the ticket booth marked *Stehplätze*—standing room. You can only buy one ticket per person (you can't buy for your spouse who's off shopping). The best tickets (if available) are in the "Parterre" section, located dead-center at stage level. Once inside, locals save their spot along the rail by tying a scarf to it. Remember,

Costumed salesmen push touristy concerts.

In Vienna, music is everywhere.

since you're a ticket holder, you can explore the rest of the opera house. No one is obligated to stay all the way until the fat lady sings, so standing room is a great way to sample a little opera.

Each spring and fall the opera projects several performances live on a huge screen on its building, puts out chairs for the public to enjoy...and it's all free. Get the schedule from the opera house website *(Oper Live am Platz)* or the *Wien-Programm* brochure.

Touristy Mozart and Strauss Concerts

A number of venues offer chamber music, played by musicians in historic costumes, in traditional settings, for about €30 to €60. Pesky wigged-and-powdered Mozarts peddle tickets in the streets. The performances may not be world-class and they're geared for tour groups, but they're generally well-done, visually interesting, and enjoyable. To sort through your options, check with the ticket office in the TI. Savvy locals suggest getting cheap tickets, and scooting up to better, unfilled seats.

Of the many fine venues in Vienna, I have two reliable favorites: The Sala Terrena at Mozarthaus (not to be confused with the Mozarthaus Vienna Museum) offers intimate chamber-music concerts (heavy on Mozart) in a Venetian Renaissance room (€49-59, Thu-Sun, near St. Stephen's Cathedral at Singerstrasse 7, tel. 01/512-3457, www.concert-in-vienna.com). The Kursalon—the hall where Johann "Waltz King" Strauss himself directed wildly popular concerts more than 100 years ago—now hosts fun evenings mixing waltzes, ballet, and music (€42-65, nightly, Johannesgasse 33 at corner of Parkring, tram #2: Weihburggasse or U: Stadtpark, tel. 01/512-5790 or www.soundofvienna.at).

Opera can be pricey...

...or free, with the live video feed.

Sightseeing After Dark

Every night in Vienna some sights stay open late. My Vienna City Walk and Ringstrasse Tram Tour both work well at night, amid floodlit monuments.

St. Stephen's Cathedral: Nightly until 22:00 (but main nave closes earlier). See page 33.

Kunst Haus Wien: Nightly until 18:00. See page 135.

Haus der Musik: Nightly until 22:00. See page 128.

Albertina Museum: Wednesday until 21:00. See page 124.

Natural History Museum: Wednesday until 21:00. See page 129.

Kunsthistorisches Museum: Thursday until 21:00. See page 129.

Vienna Boys' Choir (Wiener Sängerknaben)

The boys sing (from a high balcony, heard but not seen) at the 9:15 Sunday Mass from mid-September through June in the Hofburg's Imperial Music Chapel (Hofmusikkapelle). Reserved seats (€10-36) must be booked in advance: email office@hofmusikkapelle.gv.at (info-only tel. 01/533-9927, www.hofmusikkapelle.gv.at). Standing room inside is free for the first 60 who line up, and the rest can listen and watch a video feed for free from the narthex. The boys also perform in September and October at the MuTh concert hall (www.muth.at, tickets@muth.at).

Other Musical Options

For less serious operettas and musicals, try the Vienna Volksoper, located along the Gürtel, west of the city center (Währinger Strasse 78, tel. 01/5144-43670, get schedule at the TI, in *Wien-Programm* or www.volksoper.at). The venerable, intimate Theater an der Wien (from 1801) present operas—generally Mozart with a modern twist—and runs through the summer (facing the Naschmarkt at Linke Wienzeile 6, tel. 01/58885, www.theater-wien.at). Modern Broadway-style musicals (in German) play at several venues. You can buy advance tickets online (€10-110, Wien Ticket, tel. 01/58885, www.wien-ticket.at); discounted day-of-show tickets are sometimes available after 14:00 at the Wien Ticket pavilion next to the opera house.

Evening "Scenes"

Vienna is a great place to just be out and about on a balmy evening amid bars, cafés, trendy restaurants, and theaters. The obvious choice is the **historic center** around St. Stephen's Cathedral and the Graben. **Donaukanal** (the Danube Canal) is especially popular in the summer for

The Kursalon combines music and dance.

Hear Mozart hits in atmospheric settings.

its imported beaches. At the **Naschmarkt,** after the produce stalls close up, the bars and eateries are packed with noshing locals (see page 132). At the **MuseumsQuartier** and Spittelberg you're surrounded by far-out museums and youth-oriented bars with local students filling the courtyard (see page 130). The **Prater** amusement park attracts families and fun (see page 139). The **wine gardens** *(Heurigen)* north of downtown are a fun getaway (see page 141).

A convivial, free-to-everyone people scene erupts each evening in summer (July-Aug) on Rathausplatz, the welcoming park in front of **City Hall** (right on the Ringstrasse). Thousands of people keep a food circus of simple stalls busy. When darkness falls, everyone takes a seat on comfy benches to enjoy a movie (often with a classical-music theme) projected on a huge screen, with the City Hall's Neo-Gothic facade as a backdrop. Get the schedule at the TI or www.filmfestival-rathausplatz.at.

Balls and Waltzing

Renowned for its ball scene, Vienna boasts hundreds of balls each year, where the classic dance is the waltz. The height of ball season falls generally between December and February, when Viennese and visitors of all ages dress up and swirl to music ranging from waltzes to jazz to contemporary beats. Balls are put on by the Vienna Philharmonic, Vienna Boys' Choir, Vienna State Opera, and others (search for events at www.events.wien.info).

English Cinema

Three movie houses offer nightly English film for around €8 to €9. English Cinema Haydn is near my recommended hotels on Mariahilfer Strasse (Mariahilfer Strasse 57, tel. 01/587-2262, www.haydnkino.at). Artis International Cinema is right in the town center a few minutes from the cathedral (Schultergasse 5, tel. 01/535-6570). Burg Kino—a block from the opera house—often shows *The Third Man,* set in postwar Vienna's shadowy Cold War world (usually Sun afternoon, Fri evening, and Tue evening, Opernring 19, tel. 01/587-8406, www.burgkino.at).

Guided Tours

TI Walking Tours: A basic 1.5-hour "Vienna at First Glance" introductory walk is offered daily throughout the summer (€16, leaves at 14:00 from in front of the main TI, just behind the opera house, in English and German, just show up, tel. 01/774-8901, mobile 0664-260-4388, www.wienguide.at).

On summer evenings, enjoy take-out food…   …and classical music at the City Hall.

"Free" Walking Tour: Good Vienna Tours offers a "pay what you like" 2.5-hour walk through the city center. Reserve online or just show up (pay what you think it's worth at the end—no coins, paper only, daily departures at 10:00 and 14:00, meet at fountain at tip of Albertina across from TI, www.goodviennatours.eu).

Bike Tours: Pedal Power covers the central district in three hours, daily May to September (€29, includes bike, tel. 01/729-7234, www.pedalpower.at).

Bus Tours: Of the several companies, I like Red Bus City Tours—a 1.5-hour loop of city highlights on a convertible-top bus, with recorded commentary, including a 20-minute shopping break in the middle. Besides the Ringstrasse, they get out to Prater Park and Danube Island. Tours start at the TI on Albertinaplatz (€15 ticket from driver, several departures daily year round, tel. 01/512-4030, www.redbuscitytours.at).

Tram Tour: The Vienna Ring Tram *(VRT Ring-Rund Sightseeing),* a yellow made-for-tourists streetcar, runs clockwise along the entire Ringstrasse (starting at Schwedenplatz) in a 30-minute loop, with re-corded commentary (€9, 2/hour 10:00-17:30, www.wienerlinien.at). My Ringstrasse Tram Tour is cheaper (see page 49).

Horse-and-Buggy Tours: These traditional horse-and-buggies, called *Fiaker,* take rich romantics on clip-clop tours lasting 20 minutes (Old Town-€55), 40 minutes (Old Town and the Ring-€80), or one hour (even more thorough-€110). You can split the cost with up to five people. Because it's a kind of guided tour, chat with a few drivers to find one who's fun and speaks English (tel. 01/401-060).

Local Guides: You'll pay about €150 to €160 for two hours. (Get a group together and call it a party.) The TI website (www.vienna.info) has a long list of local guides with their specialties and contact information.

Here are my favorites: **Wolfgang Höfler** is a generalist who has fun with history and can also do bike tours (€160/2 hours, mobile 0676-304-4940, www.vienna-aktivtours.com). **Lisa Zeiler** is a good storyteller (€150/2-3 hours, mobile 0699-1203-7550, lisa.zeiler@gmx.at). **Adrienn Bartek-Rhomberg** offers themed walks, see website (€150/3 hours, mobile 0650-826-6965, www.experionce-vienna.at). **Gerhard Strassgschwandtner** is passionate about history (€160/2 hours, mobile 0676-475-7818, www.special-vienna.com).

RESOURCES FROM RICK STEVES

This Pocket guide is one of dozens of titles in my series of guidebooks on European travel. I also produce a public television series, *Rick Steves' Europe,* and a public radio show, *Travel with Rick Steves.* My website, www.ricksteves.com, offers a wealth of free travel information, including videos and podcasts of my shows and classes, audio tours of Europe's great sights, travel forums, guidebook updates, my travel blog, and my guide to European rail passes—plus an online travel store and information on our tours of Europe.

How Was Your Trip? You can share your tips, concerns, and discoveries at www.ricksteves.com/feedback. I value your feedback. Thanks in advance.

German Survival Phrases for Austria

When using the phonetics, pronounce ī as the long I sound in "light."

English	German	Phonetics
Good day.	Grüss Gott.	GREWS gote
Do you speak English?	Sprechen Sie Englisch?	SHPREHKH-ehn zee EHGN-lish
Yes. / No.	Ja. / Nein.	yah / nīn
I (don't) understand.	Ich verstehe (nicht).	ikh fehr-SHTAY-heh (nikht)
Please.	Bitte.	BIT-teh
Thank you.	Danke.	DAHNG-keh
I'm sorry.	Es tut mir leid.	ehs toot meer līt
Excuse me.	Entschuldigung.	ehnt-SHOOL-dig-oong
(No) problem.	(Kein) Problem.	(kīn) proh-BLAYM
(Very) good.	(Sehr) gut.	(zehr) goot
Goodbye.	Auf Wiedersehen.	owf VEE-der-zayn
one / two	eins / zwei	īns / tsvī
three / four	drei / vier	drī / feer
five / six	fünf / sechs	fewnf / zehkhs
seven / eight	sieben / acht	ZEE-behn / ahkht
nine / ten	neun / zehn	noyn / tsayn
How much is it?	Wieviel kostet das?	VEE-feel KOHS-teht dahs
Write it?	Schreiben?	SHRĪ-behn
Is it free?	Ist es umsonst?	ist ehs oom-ZOHNST
Included?	Inklusive?	in-kloo-ZEE-veh
Where can I buy / find...?	Wo kann ich kaufen / finden...?	voh kahn ikh KOW-fehn / FIN-dehn
I'd like / We'd like...	Ich hätte gern / Wir hätten gern...	ikh HEH-teh gehrn / veer HEH-tehn gehrn
...a room.	...ein Zimmer.	in TSIM-mer
...a ticket to ___.	...eine Fahrkarte nach ___.	Ī-neh FAR-kar-teh nahkh
Is it possible?	Ist es möglich?	ist ehs MUR-glikh
Where is...?	Wo ist...?	voh ist
...the train station	...der Bahnhof	dehr BAHN-hoht
...the bus station	...der Busbahnhof	dehr BOOS-bahn-hohf
...the tourist information office	...das Touristen-informations-buro	dahs too-RIS-tehn-in-for-maht-see-OHNS BEW roh
...the toilet	die Toilette	dee toh-LEH-tch
men	Herren	HEHR-rehn
women	Damen	DAH-mehn
left / right	links / rechts	links / rehkhts
straight	geradeaus	geh-RAH-deh-OWS
What time does this open / close?	Um wieviel Uhr wird hier geöffnet / geschlossen?	oom VEE-feel oor veerd heer geh-URF-neht / geh-SHLOH-schn
At what time?	Um wieviel Uhr?	oom VEE-feel oor
Just a moment.	Moment.	moh-MEHNT
now / soon / later	jetzt / bald / später	yehtst / bahld / SHPAY-ter

Practicalities

In the Restaurant

English	German	Pronunciation
I'd like / We'd like...	Ich hätte gern / Wir hätten gern...	ikh HEH-teh gehrn / veer HEH-tehn gehrn
...a reservation for...	...eine Reservierung für...	Ī-neh reh-zer-FEER-oong fewr
...a table for one / two.	...einen Tisch für eine Person / zwei Personen.	Ī-nehn tish fewr Ī-neh pehr- zohn / tsvī pehr-zohnehn
Non-smoking.	Nichtraucher.	NIKHT-rowkh-er
Is this seat free?	Ist hier frei?	ist heer frī
Menu (in English), please.	Speisekarte (auf Englisch), bitte.	SHPĪ-zeh-kar-teh (owf EHNG-lish) BIT-teh
service (not) included	Trinkgeld (nicht) inklusive	TRINK-gehlt (nikht) in-kloo-ZEE-veh
cover charge	Eintritt	ĪN-trit
to go	zum Mitnehmen	tsoom MIT-nay-mehn
with / without	mit / ohne	mit / OH-neh
and / or	und / oder	oont / OH-der
menu (of the day)	(Tages-) Karte	(TAH-gehs-) KAR-teh
set meal for tourists	Touristenmenü	too-RIS-tehn-meh-NEW
specialty of the house	Spezialität des Hauses	SHPAYT-see-ah-lee-TAYT dehs HOW-zehs
appetizers	Vorspeise	FOR-shpī-zeh
bread / cheese	Brot / Käse	broht / KAY-zeh
sandwich	Sandwich	ZAHND-vich
soup	Suppe	ZUP-peh
salad	Salat	zah-LAHT
meat	Fleisch	flīsh
poultry	Geflügel	geh-FLEW-gehl
fish	Fisch	fish
seafood	Meeresfrüchte	MEH-rehs-FREWKH-teh
fruit	Obst	ohpst
vegetables	Gemüse	geh-MEW-zeh
dessert	Nachspeise	NAHKH-shpī-zeh
mineral water	Mineralwasser	min-eh-RAHL-vah-ser
tap water	Leitungswasser	LĪ-toongs-vah-ser
milk	Milch	milkh
(orange) juice	(Orangen-) Saft	(oh-RAHN-zhehn-) zahft
coffee / tea	Kaffee / Tee	kah-FAY / tay
wine	Wein	vīn
red / white	rot / weiß	roht / vīs
glass / bottle	Glas / Flasche	glahs / FLAH-sheh
beer	Bier	beer
Cheers!	Prost!	prohst
More. / Another.	Mehr. / Noch eins.	mehr / nohkh īns
The same.	Das gleiche.	dahs GLĪKH-eh
Bill, please.	Rechnung, bitte.	REHKH-noong BIT-teh
tip	Trinkgeld	TRINK-gehlt
Delicious!	Lecker!	LEHK-er

For more user-friendly German phrases, check out *Rick Steves' German Phrase Book and Dictionary* or *Rick Steves' French, Italian & German Phrase Book*.

INDEX

Start your trip at

Our website enhances this book and turns

Explore Europe

At ricksteves.com you can browse through thousands of articles, videos, photos and radio interviews, plus find a wealth of money-saving travel tips for planning your dream trip. And with our mobile-friendly website, you can easily access all this great travel information anywhere you go.

TV Shows

Preview the places you'll visit by watching entire half-hour episodes of Rick Steves' Europe (choose from all 100 shows) on-demand, for free.

ricksteves.com

your travel dreams into affordable reality

Radio Interviews

Enjoy ready access to Rick's vast library of radio interviews covering

travel tips and cultural insights that relate specifically to your Europe travel plans.

Travel Forums

Learn, ask, share! Our online community of savvy travelers is a great resource for first-time travelers to Europe, as well as seasoned pros. You'll find forums on each country, plus travel tips and restaurant/hotel reviews. You can even ask one of our well-traveled staff to chime in with an opinion.

Travel News

Subscribe to our free Travel News e-newsletter, and get monthly updates from Rick on what's happening in Europe.

Audio Europe™

Rick's Free Travel App

Get your FREE Rick Steves Audio Europe™ app to enjoy…

- Dozens of self-guided tours of Europe's top museums, sights and historic walks
- Hundreds of tracks filled with cultural insights and sightseeing tips from Rick's radio interviews
- All organized into handy geographic playlists
- For Apple and Android

With Rick whispering in your ear, Europe gets even better.

Find out more at ricksteves.com

Pack Light and Right

Gear up for your next adventure at ricksteves.com

Light Luggage

Pack light and right with Rick Steves' affordable, custom-designed rolling carry-on bags, backpacks, day packs and shoulder bags.

Accessories

From packing cubes to moneybelts and beyond, Rick has personally selected the travel goodies that will help your trip go smoother.

Shop at ricksteves.com

Rick Steves has

Experience maximum Europe

Save time and energy

This guidebook is your independent-travel toolkit. But for all it delivers, it's still up to you to devote the time and energy it takes to manage the preparation and logistics that are essential for a happy trip. If that's a hassle, there's a solution.

Rick Steves Tours

A Rick Steves tour takes you to Europe's most interesting places with great guides and small groups

great tours, too!

with minimum stress

of 28 or less. We follow Rick's favorite itineraries, ride in comfy buses, stay in family-run hotels, and bring you intimately close to the Europe you've traveled so far to see. Most importantly, we take away the logistical headaches so you can focus on the fun.

Join the fun

This year we'll take thousands of free-spirited travelers—nearly half of them repeat customers—along with us on four dozen different itineraries, from Ireland to Italy to Istanbul. Is a Rick Steves tour the right fit for your travel dreams? Find out at ricksteves.com, where you can also request Rick's latest tour catalog.

Europe is best experienced with happy travel partners. We hope you can join us.

See our itineraries at ricksteves.com

A Guide for Every Trip

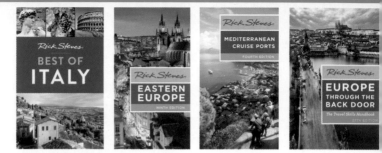

BEST OF GUIDES

*Full color easy-to-scan format,
focusing on Europe's most
popular destinations and sights.*

Best of England
Best of Europe
Best of France
Best of Germany
Best of Ireland
Best of Italy
Best of Spain

COMPREHENSIVE GUIDES

*City, country, and regional guides
with detailed coverage for a multi-week
trip exploring iconic sights and more.*

Amsterdam & the Netherlands
Barcelona
Belgium: Bruges, Brussels,
  Antwerp & Ghent
Berlin
Budapest
Croatia & Slovenia

Eastern Europe
England
Florence & Tuscany
France
Germany
Great Britain
Greece: Athens
  & the Peloponnese
Iceland
Ireland
Istanbul
Italy
London
Paris
Portugal
Prague & the Czech Republic
Provence & the French Riviera
Rome
Scandinavia
Scotland
Spain
Switzerland
Venice
Vienna, Salzburg & Tirol

Rick Steves guidebooks are published by Avalon Travel,
an imprint of Perseus Books, a Hachette Book Group company.

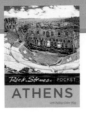

POCKET GUIDES

Amsterdam
Athens
Barcelona
Florence
Italy's Cinque Terre
London

Munich & Salzburg
Paris
Prague
Rome
Venice
Vienna

SNAPSHOT GUIDES

Focused single-destination coverage.

Basque Country: Spain & France
Copenhagen & the Best of Denmark
Dublin
Dubrovnik
Edinburgh
Hill Towns of Central Italy
Krakow, Warsaw & Gdansk
Lisbon
Loire Valley
Madrid & Toledo
Milan & the Italian Lakes District
Naples & the Amalfi Coast
Northern Ireland
Normandy
Norway
Reykjavik
Sevilla, Granada & Southern Spain
St. Petersburg, Helsinki & Tallinn
Stockholm

CRUISE PORTS GUIDES

Reference for cruise ports of call.

Mediterranean Cruise Ports
Scandinavian & Northern European
 Cruise Ports

TRAVEL SKILLS & CULTURE

Europe 101
European Christmas
European Easter
European Festivals
Europe Through the Back Door
Postcards from Europe
Travel as a Political Act

PHRASE BOOKS & DICTIONARIES

French
French, Italian & German
German
Italian
Portuguese
Spanish

PLANNING MAPS

Britain, Ireland & London
Europe
France & Paris
Germany, Austria & Switzerland
Ireland
Italy
Spain & Portugal

Rick Steves books are available from your favorite bookseller.
Many guides are available as ebooks.

PHOTO CREDITS

Avalon Travel
An imprint of Perseus Books
A Hachette Book Group company
1700 Fourth Street
Berkeley, CA 94710

Printed in China by RR Donnelley
Second Edition
Second printing September 2018

ISBN 978-1-63121-630-5

For the latest on Rick's lectures, guidebooks, tours, public radio show, and public television series, contact Rick Steves' Europe, 130 Fourth Avenue North, Edmonds, WA
98020, tel. 425/771-8303, www.ricksteves.com, rick@ricksteves.com.

Rick Steves' Europe
Managing Editor: Jennifer Madison Davis
Special Publications Manager: Risa Laib
Editors: Glenn Eriksen, Tom Griffin, Katherine Gustafson, Suzanne Kotz, Cathy Lu,
Carrie Shepherd
Editorial & Production Assistant: Jessica Shaw
Researcher: Gretchen Strauch
Graphic Content Director: Sandra Hundacker
Maps & Graphics: David C. Hoerlein, Lauren Mills, Mary Rostad

Avalon Travel
Senior Editor and Series Manager: Madhu Prasher
Editor: Jamie Andrade
Associate Editor: Sierra Machado
Editorial Intern: Rachael Sablik
Copy Editor: Maggie Ryan
Proofreader: Patty Mon
Indexer: Stephen Callahan
Production & Typesetting: Christine Del orenzo
Cover Design: Kimberly Glyder Design
Maps & Graphics: Kat Bennett

ABOUT THE AUTHORS

Rick Steves

Since 1973, Rick has spent about four months a year exploring Europe. His mission: to empower Americans to have European trips that are fun, affordable, and culturally broadening. Rick produces a best-selling guidebook series, a public television series, and a public radio show, and organizes small-group tours that take over 20,000 travelers to Europe annually. He does all of this with the help of a hardworking, well-traveled staff of 100 at Rick Steves' Europe in Edmonds, Washington, near Seattle. When not on the road, Rick is active in his church and with advocacy groups focused on economic justice, drug policy reform, and ending hunger. To recharge, Rick plays piano, relaxes at his family cabin in the Cascade Mountains, and spends time with his partner Trish, son Andy, and daughter Jackie. Find out more about Rick at www.ricksteves.com and on Facebook.

Gene Openshaw

Gene has co-authored a dozen *Rick Steves* books, specializing in writing walks and tours of Europe's cities, museums, and cultural sights. He also contributes to Rick's public television series, produces tours for Rick Steves Audio Europe, and is a regular guest on Rick's public radio show. Outside of the travel world, Gene has co-authored *The Seattle Joke Book.* As a composer, Gene has written a full-length opera called *Matter* (soundtrack available on Amazon), a violin sonata, and dozens of songs. He lives near Seattle with his daughter, enjoys giving presentations on art and history, and roots for the Mariners in good times and bad.

FOLDOUT COLOR MAP

The foldout map on the opposite page includes:
- A map of Vienna on one side
- Greater Vienna and Public Transportation map on the other side